DEREGULATION OF EXPRESS COACH SERVICES IN BRITAIN

Oxford Studies in Transport

Series editor: P. B. Goodwin

This series incorporates reports of research work undertaken at or in association with the Oxford University Transport Studies Unit, in the fields of travel behaviour and transport operations and policy. In addition, from time to time appropriate conference proceedings and other related work will be published.

Deregulation of Express Coach Services in Britain

RUSSELL P. KILVINGTON
Transport Studies Unit
University of Oxford
and
ANTHONY K. CROSS
Centre for Transport Studies
Cranfield Institute of Technology

Gower

Published by
Gower Publishing Company Limited.
Gower House, Croft Road,
Aldershot, Hampshire GU11 3HR,
England.

Gower Publishing Companv.
Old Post Road,
Brookfield,
Vermont 05036,
U.S.A.

British Library Cataloguing in Publication Data

Kilvington, Russell P.
    Deregulation of express coach services in Britain.
    —— (Oxford studies in transport)
    1. Bus lines —— Great Britain   2. Bus lines ——
    Law and legislation —— Great Britain
    I. Title   II. Cross, Anthony K.   III. Series
    388.3'22'0941   HE5663.A6

    ISBN 0-566-00873-4

Typeset on a Lasercomp at Oxford University Computing Service.

'Oxford' is a trade mark of Oxford University Press.

Printed and bound in Great Britain by
Paradigm Print, Gateshead, Tyne and Wear

CONTENTS

ACKNOWLEDGEMENTS

This report is the result of research work initiated and largely completed by the authors while part of the Transport Assessment Group in the Department of Transport Technology at Loughborough University. Its financial base, without which the work would not have been possible, was a two year research grant from the Social Science Research Council (now Economic and Social Research Council) awarded to Russell Kilvington, then lecturer in transport planning at the above University. Tony Cross was appointed as the research assistant for the project, which commenced in October 1981.

After the conclusion of Research Council sponsorship, the study was continued and finalised while the authors were respectively in post as Assistant Director of the Transport Studies Unit, Oxford University, and Research Officer, Centre for Transport Studies, Cranfield Institute of Technology. The authors acknowledge the assistance given by each of the three institutions named above in facilitating the work's continuation and conclusion.

The carrying out of this research required the cooperation of a large number of individuals and agencies. Without their willingness to be involved, the level of factual information, and consequently our understanding of the situation, would have been much reduced. We offer our grateful thanks to them all.

Special gratitude is due to all of the bus and coach operators who supplied information, participated in interviews, gave permission for and, in several cases, administered passenger surveys. At the risk of partiality, we specifically acknowledge the assistance of: A. Beetham and I. MacBriar, (National Bus Company); J. Birks and M. Pinkerton, (National Express); P. Brundle, (United Counties); W. Gunning, (Trent); B. Hogg, (B. W. Hogg); P. Jenner, (East Midlands); G. Kinch, (G. K. Kinch); T. Laver, (Boydens International); R. Nobel, (A. and W. Elsey).

We also thank R. Smalley of British Rail for allowing us access to their data on ticket sales and giving permission for the surveys of rail travellers; and F. Hill and H. Grebby of the East Midlands Traffic Commissioners office. They provided regular information on new notifications and assisted the searches made through previous licence applications.

Finally, thanks to Ann Heath and Sylvia Boyce of the Transport Studies Unit for their typing of the manuscript and their patience in setting out the numerous tabulations.

SECTION 1. INTRODUCTION AND CONTEXT

1.1 THE LEGISLATIVE CHANGE

The 1980 Transport Act invoked a new philosophy of government policy towards the bus and coach industry. This was all the more radical given that it represented a departure from a status quo of 50 years standing. The provisions of the 1930 Road Traffic Act had introduced quantity controls through a system of route (road service) licensing. This had applied to all types of service other than contract and private hire operations. A significant range of quality controls, covering aspects such as the design, safety and fitness of vehicles, licensing of drivers and conductors, etc. had also been prescribed. The latter aspect had inevitably been subject to several modifications of detail over the years. Nevertheless, the principle of public protection by regulation was as strong in 1980 as it had been during the previous five decades.

The primary aim of the new legislation was to minimize government involvement by reducing the level of regulation. Even so, control was retained in several areas. This included aspects of safety, and route licensing of stage carriage (local) services. In short, the Act sought to achieve a system of rationalisation of quality controls and, to a considerable degree, abolition of quantity control. Given this balance, it is inevitable that this study focusses most attention on the latter aspect. Some general comments on quality control are made in Section 2.4. Detailed changes such as operator licensing and annual vehicle tests are discussed in Section 3.2, which reports the views and reactions of coach operators.

The main provisions with respect to express services are contained in Sections 3 and 4 of the legislation. The distinction between express and stage carriage operation was redefined on a distance rather than a minimum fare criteria. The latter was not only inappropriate but also outdated, given that the fare level was set at a mere 21 pence. Following the 1980 Act, express services were deemed to be those where passengers were set down 30 miles or more from the place where they were taken up (measured in a straight line), or where some point on the route was 30 miles or more from the origin or destination.

1980

The most important feature regarding the operation of a newly defined express service was the removal of the need for a road service licence. All coach operators were now at liberty to enter (and leave) the market at will. This was not so in the case of stage carriage operations. Whilst some change of emphasis, designed to favour the new entrant, did take place, route licensing generally remained. The exception was trial areas. In reality, three mainly rural locations (parts of Devon, Hereford and Worcester, and Norfolk) were so designated. In these areas, quantity controls were experimentally removed. As this book goes to press, further legislation to deregulate all local bus services is expected during 1985. Although the contexts of express and stage carriage operations are clearly different, it is suggested that this study may give some indication of the likely outcome of such an event.

Express services may be divided into two categories. First, scheduled services for the carriage of passengers at separate fares. A sub-division within this is between regular frequency year round routes and summer seasonal operations. In such cases, the Act contains an obligation upon operators to notify the relevant area licensing authority, namely the Traffic Commissioners, of the intention to operate, along with details of the route and timetable. Secondly, excursions and tours travelling beyond 30 miles from any given origin - the great majority - are also categorised as express. In this instance, the definition is that of an unscheduled service offered to the public at return fares, where all passengers travel together for the whole trip. No obligation to notify the Traffic Commissioners is imposed. For the purpose of this report, we adopt the accepted categorisation of the above as simply 'express' and 'excursions and tours' respectively.

It was generally considered that the Act would have the effect of considerably increasing the freedom of entry into the industry, and into the deregulated sectors in particular. This would encourage a competitive rather than a controlled environment. It was the Conservative Government's expectation that this would provide a better level of service to the travelling public.

Speaking at a conference shortly after the enactment (The 1980 Transport Act, May Fair Hotel, London), the then Secretary of State for Transport, the Rt. Hon. Norman Fowler, explained that his legislation had three main aims. These were:

  i the removal of bureaucratic restriction
  ii the need to ensure that almost everyone gains good access to public transport
  iii the provision of maximum choice to the user, by facilitating competition.

It was hoped that deregulation would: encourage the private sector; increase the responsiveness of all operators; create new life where, previously, little had existed (this point relating especially to rural areas). Many analogies and, indeed, hopes of such achievement were drawn from the (then) success of Laker Airways. However unfortunate such a comparison may now appear in retrospect, it was nonetheless an apt one. Quite simply, the 1980 Act removed a system of regulation which had endured for half a century and created a new environment conducive to overt competition on long distance coach services.

1.2 THE RESEARCH UNDERTAKEN

Deregulation after such a long period of stability meant that operators were faced with a situation which they had not previously experienced. As such, both expectation and uncertainty within the industry was considerable. The former was inclined more towards foreboding, almost paranoia, than excitement and opportunity. Notwithstanding this, it was recognised that the nature of the legislation offered the greatest potential for change in the express and excursions and tours markets.

This study reviews the first three years of development following deregulation in these sectors. Most of the detailed information contained herein relates to the East Midlands region. This area includes the counties of Derbyshire, Leicestershire, Lincolnshire, Northamptonshire and Nottinghamshire. Industrially and commercially, the region conforms to the national average. There is an adequate mix of population density - the major cities and industrial areas of the western portion contrasted by extensive rural areas in the east. Overall density is slightly lower, whilst car ownership and personal incomes are generally higher than in other regions. Journey characteristics reflect the national average, particularly for journeys beyond 25 miles as tabulated in the Long Distance Travel Surveys. Finally, taking into account the mix of transport links - good rail and motorway links in the west but poor communications in the east - it is suggested that the East Midlands is a suitably representative area to act as a proxy for the country as a whole.

For the purpose of this study, specific consideration is given to coach services which have their origin and/or operators based in the East Midlands. This has meant the exclusion of some services originating in other regions which may terminate or pass through the study area. An exception is the analysis of all National Express routes which pick up or set down within the region. This approach is not considered to bias the findings.

From an early point in the analysis, it was found that rigid adherence to the definition of express contained within the Act might be misleading. There exist several limited stop long distance services within the region which are clearly express in spirit, albeit operated under stage carriage licence. These are included in the analysis. Similarly, a small number of excursions which are less than 30 miles in length will be contained within the statistics.

The project sought to clarify the impact of the legislation upon a variety of agencies. The removal of controls affected coach operators, existing and potential coach passengers, and public transport operators and travellers in other sectors of the transport industry. Given the level of potential interaction within the passenger travel market, it was necessary to assess the impact of a change in one sector upon the operation of another. Thus, the coach market was treated as an element in the total supply of long distance passenger transport rather than a self contained industry.

The following agencies were identified :
    i the coach operator
      a) public sector
      b) private sector
    ii the coach user
   iii the competitors, for example, British Rail, private car
    iv users of competing modes
     v other transport related bodies, for example, travel agents.

A variety of techniques and methods of analysis have been applied. Detailed explanations are contained in the appropriate sections. The investigation covers two principal areas. These are: the trends in coach operation since deregulation; and, an analysis of coach and inter-city rail users. The former category includes a detailed consideration of the events following deregulation and employs both primary and secondary techniques of data collection. Primary information and data were obtained from postal questionnaires distributed to coach operators and their travel agents, in-depth interviews with operators and related organisations, and telephone surveys. Secondary data was obtained directly from operators and relevant agencies, an analysis of the notification of express services published by the Traffic Commissioners (under a provision of the Act) and, in the case of National Express, a detailed study of changes in service frequencies, fares and patronage. The information is combined to provide a base upon which to judge the developments which have occurred.

The study of the user was undertaken by a combination of on-coach questionnaires and interviews and, in the case of British Rail, interviews conducted on railway stations in the East Midlands. A wide range of services are included, ranging from high speed motorway to relatively slow cross-country express services, along with a variety of day excursions, British and continental tours. They also vary between those provided by luxury and standard coaches and include both the nationalized and independent sectors. The variation in the nature of the services surveyed dictated specific design criteria for the questionnaire or interview.

The results of the various surveys carried out have been combined to formulate an overall impression of the experience and attitudes of users. Particular attention has been given to establishing passenger profiles and the extent to which changes in travel behaviour have arisen since deregulation.

Finally, some comments on data quality. Whilst we are personally satisfied with both the validity and representativeness of the information presented, it is obvious that detailed sampling of both operators and long distance travellers has inevitably been limited. Given this, it is of particular regret that the results stand somewhat in isolation. This is due to the conspicuous lack of accurate nationwide trends. We draw attention specifically to:

i *Changed Definitions:* The redefinition of express and stage carriage has not been compensated for in official statistics. Government transport statistics for express coach show a decline from 39 to 17 million journeys between 1980 and 1981, whereas considerable growth had taken place in the newly defined sector.

ii *Long Distance Travel Surveys:* During the 1970s, as a complement to the National Travel Survey, surveys of travel over 25 miles in journey length were conducted. Ironically, the 1979/80 survey, immediately prior to deregulation, was the last occasion on which it was administered. This very useful data source was therefore abandoned just as it was getting interesting!

iii *Excursions and Tours:* Unlike scheduled express operations, wherein there is a requirement to notify Traffic Commissioners of the intention to operate new or modified services, there is no central repository to which similar information must be declared.

1.3 OWNERSHIP AND STRUCTURE OF THE BUS AND COACH INDUSTRY

This section provides a brief account of the nature of the industry, using the East Midlands region as an example. The total picture conforms with most of Great Britain in its mix between publicly and privately owned operators. Data are presented on the size and characteristics of the firms and the types of services operated prior to deregulation. The purpose in presenting such information at this stage is to give an appropriate context to the nationwide review which follows in Section 2. Its relevance to other sections is readily apparent.

A major public sector operator is the National Bus Company. It is represented by territorial operators; namely, East Midlands, Lincolnshire Road Car, Midland Red East (now Midland Fox), Trent, and United Counties. These companies are traditionally involved in stage carriage services but also offer their own programme of excursions. A further function is the provision of vehicles and staff, along with consultation on service planning, for National Express. This subsidiary, as the name implies, possesses the overall responsibility for the planning and marketing of long distance scheduled services. However, from the summer of 1983, the responsibility for seasonal express services (normally Saturdays only to seaside destinations), was devolved in its entirety to the territorial companies. The National Bus Company is also a major operator in the tours sector through the subsidiary National Holidays. Much of this operation has grown out of the acquisition over the years of specialist coach firms. Thus, whilst holidays may be booked to commence from any part of the country, the absence of such an operator based within the East Midlands region weakens their local presence by comparison with some other areas.

Six local authorities in the East Midlands possess their own municipal bus undertakings. These are based at Chesterfield, Derby, Leicester, Lincoln, Northampton and Nottingham. Their traditional concern has been almost exclusively with stage carriage services. As will be related subsequently, growing interest is now being taken in the excursions and tours market following deregulation, in common with many municipal operators throughout the country. Table 1 contains statistics relating to these types of operator. Note the large size of these concerns, but also the relative insignificance of coaching vehicles.

Table 1

National Bus Company and Municipal Undertakings in the East Midlands

	Buses		Coaches
	Double Deck	**Single Deck**	
National Bus Company:			
East Midlands	143	114	9
Lincolnshire	89	101	35
Trent	135	224	15
Midland Red *	94	685	83
United Counties	198	264	40
Municipal Undertakings:			
Chesterfield	70	52	1
Derby	154+		10
Leicester	175	37	9
Lincoln	25	24	0
Northampton	46	34	0
Nottingham	319	43	6

Source: The Little Red Book (Ian Allan, 1982)

Notes: * Figures relate to former structure before
              division into smaller units
            + Figures relate to all buses

By contrast, the private sector is characterised by a considerable number of small firms. In general, fleet size varies between one and ten vehicles, of which the great majority are likely to be coaches. This reflects their traditionally small scale of operation and concern with seasonal express, excursions and tours, private hire and contract services. An exception to both of these criteria is Barton Transport of Nottingham. The company owns a fleet of over 250 multi-purpose vehicles. These are utilised in the maintenance of by far the largest independent operator network of stage carriage services in Great Britain. A strong tradition is also maintained in the holiday express and excursions and tours business.

An analysis of the independent sector is shown in Tables 2 and 3. Although the source of the data is recognised as being authoritative, deficiencies in its comprehensiveness can readily be seen. Firms providing no information are likely to own only a small number of vehicles and focus on contract and private hire. Information is given on the number of firms, number of coaches owned and types of licence held prior to deregulation. It is worth considering the implications of these statistics, given the intention of the 1980 Act to stimulate this sector. It can be seen that between one and two thirds of the operators had possessed licences for express and/or excursions and tours, although such possession did not guarantee that such services were regularly operated. Equally, some services licensed in these categories prior to the 1980 Act were sometimes anomalous. For example, several works contracts, where fares were in excess of 21 pence, were classified as express. Nevertheless, the statistics suggest that considerable operating experience was already present in these areas. As a corollary, the number of firms without licences show the potential for new entrepreneurs to enter these markets after deregulation. Alternatively, one must re-emphasize the small size of these undertakings. The problems and limitations arising from such a scale of operation will come to be well recognised in the subsequent narrative.

Table 2
Independent Coach Operators in the East Midlands:
Number of Firms and Coach Ownership by County

Number of Coaches	Derby -shire	Leicester -shire	Lincoln -shire	Northampton -shire	Nottingham -shire	Total
1-2	5	1	2	3	1	12
3-4	8	7	7	5	4	31
5-6	9	6	7	3	4	29
7-8	4	6	3	3	4	20
9-10	2	4	2	1	5	14
11-12	0	2	2	1	1	6
13-14	1	1	2	0	3	7
15-16	0	2	3	0	0	5
More than 16	0	3	4	4	5	16
No information	3	3	6	3	16	31
No. of Firms	32	35	38	23	43	171

Source: The Little Red Book (1982)

Note: The data presented may be incomplete. Several
small companies may not have completed returns

Table 3
Independent Coach Operators in the East Midlands:
Analysis of Route Licences held before Deregulation

Type of Licence	Derby -shire	Leicester -shire	Lincoln -shire	Northampton -shire	Nottingham -shire
Express only	0	3	1	0	3
Express and stage	1	1	1	2	1
Express, stage and excursions/tours	4	11	17	6	6
Express and excursions/tours	5	6	1	4	3
Excursions/tours and stage	3	2	3	2	2
Excursions/tours only	6	3	2	0	3
Stage only	5	2	2	2	3
Not Stated/None *	7	7	10	7	22
Number of firms	31	35	37	23	43
% with an Express licence	32	60	54	52	30
% with an Excursions/ tours licence	58	63	62	52	33

Source: The Little Red Book (1982)

Note: *   The majority of firms in this category are small undertakings, usually specialising in contract and private hire only.

SECTION 2. REVIEW OF NATIONWIDE EVENTS

2.1 INTRODUCTION

The East Midlands was selected as the area for detailed research. It was expected that it would adequately reflect the mix of changes likely to arise throughout the country. With very few exceptions, we suggest that this has been the case. However, to enable the reader to formulate his/her own judgement and to set the analysis in a wider context, this section offers a resume of events in other areas.

This is by no means an easy task. Information deficiencies have already been mentioned in Section 1.2. This review draws upon our own primary data collection along with the published and stated views of other interested parties (operators, politicians, researchers, etc.). Although a very good appreciation of the *principal* events in the express sector can be gained, there is a significant dearth of information in the area of excursions and tours.

2.2 EXPRESS SERVICES

2.2.1 BACKGROUND

The pre 1980 Act situation was one of regulation by route licensing. It is important to understand the outcome of this system in practice. Whilst competition between coach and other modes (especially rail) was controlled, it was not prevented. By comparison with most European countries, a very comprehensive express coach system was operated, some of the main characteristics of which can be summarised as follows:

a) Dominance of year round services by publicly owned operators

Although National Express and the Scottish Bus Group carried fewer than 10 million passengers within a total of 39 million express passenger journeys in 1980 (Department of Transport, 1981), they provided the only network of year round services. Indeed, only a very small number of independents operated any long distance inter-city routes. Their major role was related to the provision of seasonal holiday services during the summer period.

b) Extensive network of places served

Year round and seasonal services both offered a more comprehensive range of origins and destinations than the rail network. Seasonal services were often characterised by several local pick up points followed by a relatively direct run to the destination. The year round services generally exhibited slow operating speeds, a large number of pick up and set down points, indirect routeing and limited frequency. Relatively limited use was made of motorway routes. As an example, Illustration 1 shows the National Express timetable between Manchester and London in 1978.

c) Relatively low fare levels

Even before deregulation, the key factor in public awareness of coach travel was the low level of fare. In general, these were around 50-75% of the normal rail tariff. This requires further clarification. During the latter part of the 1970s British Rail's increasingly sophisticated market pricing had been eroding this balance in some areas. Two examples were the student railcard, offering half price travel, and the Big City Saver special discount fare available on certain Anglo-Scottish off peak services.

d) Low market share

The 1979/80 Long Distance Travel Surveys credited 'ordinary or express bus' with a 2% share of journeys within Great Britain in excess of 25 miles. Excursions and tours were of the same magnitude whilst private hire and contract held 3%. Not surprisingly, car was the dominant mode with 78%, whilst rail's share was 14% (Department of Transport, 1981).

e) A declining market

Official statistics are slightly difficult to interpret due to changes in the definition of express services between 1971/72 and 1976/77. Even so, it is clear that the period 1970-80 had seen a decline in express service patronage (measured in passenger journeys). This reduction appears to have been somewhat greater than the 28% fall in stage carriage loadings for the same period (Department of Transport, 1981). The trend is very evident in figures relating to National Express. These show a fall from 13 million in 1975 to just 10.4 million passenger journeys in 1979. A further decline of 17% was recorded in the first 9 months of 1980 by comparison with 1979 (Birks, 1983).

NATIONAL EXPRESS »

Table 472		Table 472

800	**Manchester** – ALTRINCHAM – **London**	800
801	**Manchester** – STOCKPORT – BUXTON – DERBY – **London**	801
802	**Rochdale** – OLDHAM – MANCHESTER – STOCKPORT – MACCLESFIELD – HANLEY – BIRMINGHAM – **London**	802
803	**Manchester** – STOCKPORT – **London**	803
805	**Manchester** – ALTRINCHAM – BIRMINGHAM – COVENTRY – **London**	805
806	**Manchester** – ALTRINCHAM – WOLVERHAMPTON – **Birmingham**	806
807	**Rochdale** – OLDHAM – MANCHESTER – STOCKPORT – WYTHENSHAWE – LUTON – **London**	807

Showing complete service between Manchester and London including part Services 804, 809 and 905

	803	800	802	905	801	805	807	800	806	803	809	809	804
Periods of operation											1		
Days of operation	ThFSSu	D	D	D	D	D	D	D	FSSuM	ThFSSu	FSSu	D	D
ROCHDALE, Yellowey Coach Stn., Weir St........	....	....	0810	....	....	....	1410	....	....	....	....	....	2225
Rochdale, opp. 256 Milnrow Rd	....	....	0813	....	....	....	1413	....	....	....	....	....	2228
Milnrow, jct. Dale St./Kiln Lane....................	....	....	0816	....	....	....	1416	....	....	....	....	....	2231
Newhey, 249 Newhey Rd...............................	....	....	0819	....	....	....	1419	....	....	....	....	....	2234
Shaw, opp. 40 Market St................................	....	....	0824	....	....	....	1424	....	....	....	....	....	2239
OLDHAM, Yellowey Coach Stn., 3 Mumps	....	....	0835	....	....	....	1435	....	....	....	....	....	2250
Hollinwood, opp. 686 Manchester Rd.........	....	....	0842	....	....	....	1442	....	....	....	....	....	2257
Failsworth, Pole	....	....	0844	....	....	....	1444	....	....	....	....	....	2258
MANCHESTER, National Coach Stn., Chorlton St.. arr.	....	....	0905	....	....	....	1505	....	....	....	....	....	2320
MANCHESTER, National Coach Stn., Chorlton St. dep.	0715	0815	0915	1000	1115	1315	1515	1715	1800	1815	2330	2330	2330
Stretford, opp. St. Matthew's Church............	....	0830	....	1015	....	1330	....	1730	1815	....	....	2352	2352
Sale, opp. Odeon Cinema, nr. School Rd.......	....	0835	....	1020	....	1335	....	1735	1820	....	....	2356	2356
ALTRINCHAM, Interchange Bus Stn	....	0844	....	1029	....	1344	....	1744	1829	....	....	0004	0004
STOCKPORT, Mersey Sq............................	0735	....	0935	....	1135	....	1535	....	....	1835	2350	2350	....
Sherston, Royal Thorn Hotel	0745	....	....	....	....	....	....	....	....	1845	....	....	....
WYTHENSHAWE, Town Centre, Rowlandsway	0758	0856	....	....	....	....	1547	....	....	....	....	....	....
Over Tabley, Church...................................	....	....	....	....	....	1356	1601	1756	1841	1858	....	....	....
MACCLESFIELD, Bus Stn	....	....	1005	....	....	....	....	....	....	....	0020	0020	....
Leek, Bus Stn	....	....	1036	....	....	....	....	....	....	....	0052	0052	....
HANLEY, Bus Stn	....	....	1102	....	....	....	....	....	1915	....	....	....	0115
NEWCASTLE-U-LYME, School St.............	....	....	....	1209	....	....	....	....	....	....	....	....	0125
Disley, Rams Head Hotel..........................	....	....	....	....	1152	....	....	....	....	....	....	....	....
New Mills, Swan Hotel	....	....	....	....	1155	....	....	....	....	....	....	....	....
Whaley Bridge, Rail Stn	....	....	....	....	1200	....	....	....	....	....	....	....	....
BUXTON, Market Pl...................................	....	....	....	....	1220	....	....	....	....	....	....	....	....
Ashbourne, Bus Stn	....	....	....	....	1300	....	....	....	....	....	0123	0123	....
DERBY, Bus Stn., The Morledge	....	....	....	....	1335	....	....	....	....	....	0151	0151	....
WOLVERHAMPTON, Coach Stn., Faulkland St	....	....	....	1313	....	....	....	....	2002	....	....	....	0320
Dudley, Bus Stn	....	....	....	1330	....	....	....	....	2016	....	....	....	0338
Bearwood, Kings Head Bus Bay	....	....	....	1347	....	....	....	....	2030	....	....	....	....
BIRMINGHAM, Digbeth Coach Stn ⟵ arr.	....	....	1235	1357	....	1516	....	....	2040	....	....	....	0406
BIRMINGHAM, Digbeth Coach Stn ⟵ dep.	....	....	1240	1407	....	1521	....	....	....	....	....	....	0406
Bickenhill, W.M.P.T.E. Bus Stop nr jct. A45/M42	....	....	....	....	....	*	....	....	....	....	....	....	*
COVENTRY, Pool Meadow .... arr.	....	....	....	....	....	1605	....	....	....	....	....	....	0449
COVENTRY, Pool Meadow .... dep.	....	....	....	....	....	1610	....	....	....	....	....	....	0449
LUTON, Bute St. Bus Stn	....	....	....	....	....	....	1904	....	....	....	0518	0518	0634
St. Albans, 41 London Rd..........................	....	....	....	....	....	....	1930	....	....	....	0546	0546	....
North Finchley, Kingsway	....	....	....	....	....	....	2000	....	....	....	0557	0557	....
Golders Green, 650 Finchley Rd.................	....	....	....	....	....	....	2011	....	....	....	....	....	....
Hendon, Watford Way, Prothero Gardens......	1127	1225	1440	....	1620	1824	....	2125	....	2227	....	....	0707
LONDON, King's Cross, Pancras Rd., Nat. Exp. Stop	....	....	....	....	....	....	2034	....	....	....	0617	0617	....
LONDON, Victoria Coach Stn. ⟵	1152	1250	1505	1835	1645	1849	2059	2150	....	2252	0647	0647	0730

COACHMASTERS ARE
VALID ON THESE SERVICES

CODE 1   Daily 3 July to 7 September 1978.
For full details of Service 804 Rochdale – Manchester – London night service see Table 473.
For full details of Service 809 Bacup – Manchester – London night service see Table 473.
For full details of Service 905 Colne – Manchester – London see Table 516.
Connections are available at St. Albans and Luton with London Country (Greenline) Service 727 to Gatwick, Heathrow and Luton Airports.
All services observe a refreshment halt en route.
FOR A SUMMARY OF CONNECTIONS AT BIRMINGHAM, SEE TABLE 471
FOR A SUMMARY OF SERVICES BETWEEN THE POTTERIES, BIRMINGHAM, LONDON, SEE TABLE 371

For explanation of standard notes see introduction.

Illustration 1: A typical National Express timetable in 1978

2.2.2   THE EVENTS: REGULAR   FREQUENCY   LONG DISTANCE SERVICES

The removal of express route licensing was met with great enthusiasm by several coach operators, most of the press, the public, and the Government. The Minister (shortly to become Secretary of State) for Transport, attended a champagne launching of the newly formed British Coachways Consortium. This body was an association created directly in response to the legislation. At the outset, it included six of the major independent coach companies in the country. Before the end of 1980 the Consortium had grown to ten. Their objective was to establish a nationwide network of trunk routes between the major cities, travelling at high speeds and utilising the motorway network wherever possible.

The feature of the British Coachways network which caught the greatest public attention was the low level and simplicity of the fare. Offering single fares only, with no child reductions, it was based upon an extremely coarse concentric zonal system radiating from London. Thus, single fares were £2 to Birmingham, £3 to Nottingham, £4 to Liverpool etc. They represented approximately 50% of the equivalent National Express charges. There is still uncertainty as to whether such fares were intended to be genuinely promotional, or whether it was expected that profits could be made at these levels. Whatever the true picture, there was little doubt about the commitment of the operators at the time. Speaking at the May Fair Hotel conference in February 1981 (op.cit. page 2), Mr. T. McLachlan (General Manager of Grey-Green coaches; founder members of British Coachways) declared that long distance inter-urban travel at high speed, and hence high vehicle utilisation, represented one of the last remaining areas in express operations where the potential for profit was great.

Several smaller independent operators clearly held the same view. Many entered the scene, in almost all cases trying out services from their own regional base to and from London. The focus of attention upon the capital city was further intensified by the swift response of National Express and the Scottish Bus Group. The competition was matched in several ways, including price. Specifically, all of the British Coachways fare offers were equalled. Moreover, National Express was not only acting in a responsive manner. Immediately prior to deregulation it had a completed CoachMAP, a detailed market research study of its passenger market. The timetable introduced on 21 September 1980 had brought about significant changes. Faster and higher frequency services were introduced between the main centres of population, operating on the motorway network wherever possible, with little or no route diversion to intermediate stopping points. They had also gained experience of the potential for low fares through a highly successful experiment with standby fares on the Manchester-London service in July 1980. Finally, an intensive marketing campaign featuring 'Beeper the Frog' was launched.

The initial effects of deregulation were thus spectacular. An article in the trade journal Motor Transport (February 1981) quoted the Minister as stating that,

> cheap fares and good services are attracting new people onto coach services who previously might not have travelled.

The public had suddenly rediscovered the coach. By the end of 1980, National Express loadings were up by 54% on the equivalent period of the previous year, with the main routes showing astonishing expansion. MacBriar (1982) claimed a growth of 200% on the routes from London to Manchester and Birmingham for the above period. It is reasonable to assume that at least half of the new growth must have been focussed upon the trunk routes, since it was here that the majority of special low fares were on offer. Furthermore, the revision of services in September 1980 had reduced the frequency on many lower density routes and withdrawn services to several intermediate settlements.

The intense competition on the trunk routes was to be short lived. The outcome was heavily in favour of the established operators. From April 1981, members of British Coachways began to withdraw from routes and also from the consortium as such. A major blow was the departure of Grey-Green in July 1981, this being the only London based operator in the group. The dream of high profit had in reality turned into substantial loss. The whole concept of an independent network of inter-city coach routes disappeared and few of the October 1980 services now remain.

What were the reasons for failure? The positive and rapid reaction of National Express must have been a major factor. It is interesting that in Scotland, where the established operator's actions have been far less responsive to the competition, the independent sector has prospered to a greater extent. Several additional reasons for British Coachways' inability to compete have also been suggested.

Gorman (1982) considered that some basic mistakes were made in marketing. He notes that the entire operation was founded upon one advantage - price. The established operator had the goodwill of the existing market, better terminals and a better product. Certainly, it is true that no attempt was made by British Coachways to offer anything but the most basic quality of coach, whilst the derelict railway goods yard in London which became King's Cross coach station could boast few amenities.

Wilson (1982) also notes that British Coachways were unable to make themselves known to the public. Given their blaze of free publicity on entering the scene, this is at first difficult to accept. However, it is true that few travel agents were appointed and the location of pick up and set down points were not well known to passengers. This stands in stark contrast with the many thousands of travel agents who act as National Express agents and that company's ownership of major interchange terminals such as Victoria coach station. Wilson also suggests that managerial difficulties arose within the loosely bound confederation.

When one adds to all this the lower frequency of service offered by British Coachways, the lack of success was, with hindsight, inevitable. Success in a deregulated environment necessitates high entrepreneurial ability and the provision of a better or different product from that offered by an established competitor. In this context, it is interesting to review the fortunes of the smaller independents on daily trunk services.

These can best be described as mixed. The experience at one extreme has been of financial disaster. Both Glennline (Exeter-London) and North West Coachlines (Isle of Man-Lancashire-London) have ceased trading entirely, the former being a clear casualty of competition between rival coach operators (see below). Incidentally, the latter operator is one of only two bus and coach companies which we understand to have been established as a direct response to the 1980 Act. The other - Stagecoach of Perth - has, by contrast, apparently been successful.

Other independents have prospered and continue to run very much to the pattern conceived in the early days of deregulation. A smaller number have also entered the market since then, giving a total of about 15 firms. If a generalisation is sought, then the keyword for their success must be specialisation. The identification and develop-ment of just one or two routes, either inadequately or not served by the existing market, appears crucial. In route network terms these have clearly been few and far between.

Even if we include the few remnants of the British Coachways network to have survived (now operated by individual firms), a crude estimate of total journeys on independent operator services seems unlikely to be in excess of one million passengers per year. Their only significant market share is on the Anglo-Scottish routes where, uniquely, three independent companies remain in competition with the Scottish Bus Group. The above figure contrasts with a National Express 1982 total of 14 million and about 400,000 with respect to the Scottish Bus Group.

The reasons for lack of success by small undertakings are perhaps more predictable than those surrounding British Coachways. When companies seek to run outside their normal geographical territory, it is not surprising that problems arise. For example: where to pick up and set down passengers; where to sell tickets; how to judge appropriate timings for the (usually) limited frequency of service to be offered; how to become known to the public outside one's own local operating area?

The final point is particularly crucial. All operators agree that good marketing is an essential prerequisite in a deregulated environment. It explains the paradox that small operators have faced with regard to London services. It is relatively easy to generate some demand for a service *to* London from local residents (say within a catchment of 100,000). It is far more difficult to generate even the *same* level of demand from London's seven million inhabitants.

Some independents have pioneered an additional form of specialisation. This is to compete through the provision of a higher quality product. Coaches offering high levels of comfort, featuring catering, toilet and video film facilities have been introduced by operators such as Cotters (Anglo-Scottish), Flights (airport services) and Trathens (Plymouth-Exeter-London). Around half of the independents who continue to operate have adopted such an 'upmarket' approach.

The motivation for this approach is best summed up by Gorman (1982), the traffic manager of Cotters. He described the quality coach in itself as a powerful marketer of 'a new concept in a traditional market'. Their success in gaining annual patronage on their Glasgow/Edinburgh - London services in excess of 100,000 passengers per year does not rely on the British Coachways formula of low price. Cotters' fares have consistently been above those of its three coach competitors and only marginally below British Rail bargain fares. For example, the Coachline return fare in 1981 was £19.50, contrasting with the British Rail big-city saver of £20.

Gorman goes on to suggest that the development of such services represents 'the single most important change in the coaching industry since deregulation came into force'. Is this so?

It is certainly true that the introduction of high quality vehicles into express operations cannot be seen as a passing phase. This is emphasized by the response of National Express who introduced their own luxury Rapide services on major trunk routes from 1982. However, to suggest a revolution in future coach travel is perhaps premature. The following two factors should be borne in mind.

First, the question of costs. The luxury coaches in question normally have a retail price in excess of £100,000, i.e., approximately double that of a standard vehicle. This is a major cost burden to be borne, even in the context of a labour intensive industry. Clearly, vehicles should only continue to be purchased where extra revenue is generated to cover the difference in cost from operating a standard design. Our informal discussions with operators suggest that there is only a limited appreciation of the extra costs involved. Reasons for purchase seemed far more along the lines of 'because everyone else is buying them and I can't be left behind'. Moreover, it appears that the depressed nature of the coach sales market appears to be inducing manufacturers to offer many such vehicles at bargain prices. Obviously, such a situation cannot continue indefinitely. In short, this suggests a probable limitation to market penetration. This point was emphasized by Dodds (1983), during his term of office as Bus and Coach Council independent sector chairman. He asserted that:

> high specification vehicles are beyond the scope of new operators and this is a competitive disadvantage. Price cutting will force most newcomers out of business.

The second factor relates to the nature of the market. The success of Cotters illustrates that a significant number of new coach passengers can be generated. Their stated figure of 48-55% abstraction from rail is somewhat higher than the overall view of express deregulation where rail abstraction is normally put at around 30% of *new* travellers (see Section 2.2.5). Research by Kent (1984) of three other upmarket operators also suggests abstraction between 39 and 47%. If it is the case that the high quality service has a long term future, one might suggest that the passenger profile of users should be somewhat different from the user of standard vehicles. In other words, a new market is being generated. Beyond the slightly higher figure for rail abstraction, Kent's study indicates somewhat the reverse. For example, travel on company business ranged from 0 to 3% of trip purpose, whilst only 5 to 10% of travellers stated that they would have travelled by car (driver or passenger) had the coach not been available. Most significantly the dominant reason for choosing coach was, lower fare (30 to 43%), easily in excess of luxury service/entertainment at 15 to 25%.

Our conclusion on high quality services is therefore that they have made an impact on the express market. They are the most readily identifiable common factor by which the independent sector has enjoyed success. They have helped to induce a greater diversion of rail passengers to road than in the case of other express operations. Alternatively, there are two uncertainties clouding prospects for the future. These are the long term effects of the increased costs of operation, and the extent to which genuinely new coach travel markets can be established through high quality vehicles.

One further aspect of independent versus public sector coach competition should be raised, not least because it raises an apparent paradox in the nature of free competition. This is the fact that around 25% of independent operators have maintained their interest in year round long distance services by entering into joint operating agreements with National Express. In effect, the free market has regulated itself against competition. The operators are Tricentrol (Milton Keynes - London), Whittles (Bridgnorth/Kidderminster - London), Trathens (Plymouth - London), and two former members of British Coachways, Wallace Arnold and Grey Green.

The gain to National Express from this arrangement has been to restrict future competition. In the case of Trathens and Wallace Arnold they were also able to enjoy rapid access to high quality vehicles. Those of Trathens were not only deployed on Plymouth - London but were leased by National Express to launch Rapide services to Yorkshire and South Wales. The independents have gained security and the infrastructure benefits of the larger partner (terminals, travel agents, etc.). Mutual benefits have been the increased interconnection of operation (all services are advertised in a common timetable) and the establishment of a position of collective dominance which should restrain further outbreaks of competition. As an illustration of this, the Trathens/National alliance on Plymouth/Exeter - London effectively eliminated Glennline from the route. Whilst it provides an extreme example of deregulated competition, this route saw the emergence of three competitors to National immediately upon enactment (the third operator being British Coachways) only to return to one operation some 15 months later.

In conclusion, regular frequency services, having experienced a considerable level of competitive activity, have now returned to a more stable position than the other areas of express and excursions and tours to which we shall now turn. Further outbreaks of competition in the future seem unlikely, given the learning process which all operators should have either actively or passively experienced. Whittle (1983), a much respected independent operator, sums up the situation:

> unless he (any new operator) has a pot of money, he doesn't stand a chance on long distance regular express services.

2.2.3 THE EVENTS: OTHER EXPRESS OPERATIONS

Most of the attention and publicity given to deregulation has surrounded the events referred to in the previous section. As such, this has given a somewhat biassed picture of the overall situation. Only limited research has been carried out to date into commuter coaching in the London area. Equally, we are unaware of any substantial analysis of seasonal services beyond that which is documented herein for the East Midlands. Brevity of word should not therefore be construed as an adequate representation of the significance of all that has taken place in the following areas.

Commuter coaches are express operations specialising in the provision of journey to work services. Whilst some offer nothing beyond journeys in the peak, others intensify their operation at this time and maintain reasonable frequencies in the off peak. Given the requirement that passengers must travel beyond 30 miles, commuter coaching has been almost entirely confined to the Greater London area. Such operations were slow to develop following deregulation, with several failures. White (1983b) estimates about 70 vehicles per day entering London in early 1982. Even this figure appeared in jeopardy when Olsen Brothers, the major independent operator with approximately 40% of the above total, went into liquidation with debts of £500,000.

This period, perhaps fortuitously, coincided with a prolonged series of rail strikes and other operators became eager to take over the Olsen routes. A major period of expansion ensued. White (1984) suggests that the number of vehicles had reached 164 by May 1983, rising to 311 twelve months later. The 1984 figure comprises independent operators (124), municipal undertakings (27), and the

National Bus Company (160). Hence, independent operators appear to have prospered to a far greater extent in this type of operation than on the longer distance services described previously. This may reflect the more local nature of the commuter operation, serving a small pick up area, where the operator is already well known or can quickly become so. It is also true that many of the commuter services operated by independents display characteristics akin to those found in the private hire field (i.e. where the operator is likely to have existing experience). In other words, the service offered comprises a single or small number of peak journeys into the capital in the morning, returning in the evening. Vehicles are either idle or deployed on private hire or contract work during the intervening period. This contrasts with public sector commuter coach services, which tend to maintain their operation throughout the day.

As yet, there is no sign that the market has reached saturation level. Coverage still remains extremely patchy, being mainly confined to north Kent (approximately 40% of all services), north west London and Berkshire. There would appear to be a very loose correlation with ease of road access to central London and the quality of rail services (including access time to local stations), but further research is necessary to establish the precise reasons for success and failure and to assess future trends.

The rise of commuter coaching has not been great in terms of overall market share. It represents about 6% of all British Rail trips from outside the Greater London Council boundary. However, revenue loss on high cost peak operations - both to British Rail and London Transport - can hardly be seen as insignificant, especially in a market which also exhibits natural decline.

The remaining services to be discussed are best grouped together under the title of seasonal express. Largely provided by independent operators, these permit a fuller utilisation of vehicles during the summer season, and may also offer increased operating flexibility. Many undoubtedly represent 'the odd idea I've had for some time' in the mind of the operator which was not possible (or worth trying to obtain a licence for) before deregulation. Wilson (1982) confirms that many independents had expanded their range of operations in this area during the first summer following deregulation. They had built up a wider choice of destinations and a more comprehensive coverage of local area pick up points. This had often led to overlap between operators' traditional territories. Hence, the increase in terms of travel opportunity should not be exaggerated. What is undeniable is that a more competitive situation has ensued and been maintained than on regular frequency services. Not surprisingly, many operators have expressed their disquiet with the situation. Wilson also suggests that voluntary area agreements are appearing between operators in this field for their mutual benefit. This can be compared with the collaboration between National Express and certain independent operators, discussed in Section 2.2.2. A more detailed insight into the nature of this type of express service is given in Section 3.

The total number of express services launched since deregulation has therefore been considerable. In a statement to the House of Commons on 19 March 1984, the Secretary of State for Transport, the Rt. Hon. Nicholas Ridley, announced that 700 new services had commenced since deregulation, and remained scheduled (i.e. no notification of service withdrawal had been lodged. Since this procedure is known to have been ignored by many operators, the statistic should be regarded as a potential maximum figure). Notwithstanding the above, this is a significant development, especially when set against a stated total of 1,200 for the number of services running in 1980. Some care should be exercised when interpreting the absolute scale of these developments and their impact upon the travelling public. Our own estimate is that some 450 of the above must be seasonal operations. This figure is confirmed by Barton and Everest (1984). In addition, many new services can often be little more than minor alterations to former licences. Equally, many are designed to gain operating flexibility and have not necessarily commenced (following notification to the Traffic Commissioners) or have only been operated on a limited number of occasions.

2.2.4 OVERALL PERFORMANCE OF NATIONAL EXPRESS

Given the dominance of this operator in the competitive environment following deregulation, a separate record of overall achievement is presented. We concentrate upon three performance indicators - patronage, fares, and service characteristics. All of these aspects are subject to more detailed analysis and further substantiation within the East Midlands context in Section 3.3.3.

Table 4 illustrates the situation between 1980-83, revealing an increase in patronage of 75% during the period. Although 1983 appears to have been a disappointing year, allowance for the gains due to the series of rail disputes in 1982 suggests an underlying growth in patronage of 4.1%. Performance since 1980 is all the more dramatic in the context of the decline which had prevailed since 1975.

It is very important to understand that such growth has not been evenly distributed throughout the network. Spectacular increases have taken place on the major motorway routes (200% has already been noted for London to Birmingham and Manchester). This contrasts with only limited growth and in some cases decline on cross country and seasonal express services.

Table 4

National Express Performance

	1980	1981	1982	1983
Patronage (millions)	8	12	14	13.3
Revenue	£32m	£42m	£52m	£52m
Contribution to working profit	£3.1m	£4.0m	£6.0m	£3.8m
Profit, fully allocated cost	£0.1m	£0.3m	£1.6m	-£0.4m

Source: 1980-82 figures; Birks (1983).
1983 figures; National Bus Company (1984).

Such differences can also be perceived in relation to fares. Although the very low fares on trunk routes introduced immediately after deregulation have not been maintained, current average fares are still lower, even in monetary terms than in the summer of 1980. However, low fares do not apply on all routes and a great deal of selective market pricing can be found. In real terms the picture is a mixed one of fare increases, stability and bargain travel varying by route and ticket type. The impact of variations in the latter in determining the average fare level is important, especially in relation to the more recent fare changes. A considerable increase in the eligibility for bargain return fares has taken place, at the same time as some large increases in the price of single tickets.

Service characteristics also show considerable change. Trunk routes show an intensification and simplification of operation. This is a trend which has *continued* to evolve since the enactment. Illustration 2 shows the National Express timetable between Manchester and London in Autumn 1983. This should be compared with Illustration 1 in Section 2.2.1. By contrast, more limited changes in frequency can be observed on other routes, with some service reductions balancing modest increases. Cross country routes, however, do display a reorientation towards more direct limited stop characteristics. An excellent example is the Nottingham to Portsmouth link. Illustrations 3 and 4 show the service in 1980/81, initially unchanged by deregulation, and late 1983 respectively. Note how the number of stopping points between the two cities has been reduced from 49 to 15.

It should also be mentioned that new high frequency local and regional express services have been actively developed in several parts of the country. These function, in a sense, as second tier express operations, although they are apparently not designed as feeders to the primary network, nor to fill gaps created by the retrenchment of stopping points thereupon. Unfortunately, the emergence of Midlands Express, a network serving the East and West Midlands, came towards the end of our research and we were unable to undertake detailed analysis of such operations. A passenger survey on a service of a similar nature, the X67 Lincoln to Manchester, was undertaken in summer 1982 and is discussed subsequently.

The commercial success of National Express is undeniable. This has been achieved in a manner consistent with an entrepreneur acting in a laissez faire economy. In other words, concentrate on those areas offering the greatest commercial opportunity. We can identify a strong change of emphasis within this overall - picture of growth. Operations have moved away from the concept of serving the maximum possible number of locations to the concentration and development of traffic on the primary inter-urban flows. This has brought the operation more directly into competition with another provider of inter-city public transport, whose actions and performance we now discuss.

NATIONAL EXPRESS»

| 800 | Burnley/Chorley - BOLTON - MANCHESTER - **London** | 800 |

Showing full service between Manchester and London

'Rapide' service is available on journeys printed in red

	Rapide		Rapide		Rapide	
For Bank Holiday arrangements see below	540	800	540	800	540	800
Days of operation	D	D	D	D	D	ThFSSu
COLNE, Bus Stn.			0935			
Colne, 25 Albert Rd. opp. Spring Lane			0937			
Nelson, Bus Stn.			0942			
Brierfield, Bus Stop. nr. Town Hall			0945			
BURNLEY, Bus Stn.			1000			1600
Accrington, Stand O, Infant St.			1015			1615
BLACKBURN, Rail Stn., Boulevard			1030			1630
Darwen, 23 Bolton Rd.			1045			1645
CHORLEY, Bus Stn.		0830				
Atherton, Punch Bowl		0857				
BOLTON, Moor Lane Bus Stn.		0910	1110			1710
MANCHESTER, National Coach Stn., Chorlton St......arr.		0940	1140			1740
MANCHESTER, National Coach Stn., Chorlton St.....dep.	0800	1000	1200	1400	1600	1800
Corley, THF Service Area		R		R		R
LONDON, Victoria Coach Stn.	1145	1415	1545	1815	1945	2215

	Rapide			Rapide		Rapide	
For Bank Holiday arrangements see below	540	800	800	540	800	540	800
Days of operation	D	D	FSSuM	D	D	D	FSSuM
LONDON, Victoria Coach Stn.	1000	1200	1200	1400	1600	1800	2000
Corley, THF Service Area		R	R		R		R
MANCHESTER, National Coach Stn., Chorlton St......arr.	1345	1615	1615	1745	2015	2145	0015
MANCHESTER, National Coach Stn., Chorlton St.....dep.			1615	1745	2015		
BOLTON, Moor Lane Bus Stn.			1645	1815	2045		
Atherton, Punch Bowl					2058		
CHORLEY, Bus Stn.					2125		
Darwen, Belgrave Church			1705	1835			
BLACKBURN, Rail Stn., Boulevard			1720	1850			
Accrington, Stand K, Peel St.			1735	1905			
BURNLEY, Bus Stn.			1750	1920			
Brierfield, opp. Town Hall				1932			
Nelson, Bus Stn.				1935			
Colne, Albert Rd., opp. P.O.				1940			
COLNE, Bus Stn.				1942			

AGENTS MUST ALLOW AT LEAST 40 MINUTES FOR CONNECTIONS AT LONDON
For overnight service between E. Lancs, Manchester and London refer to service 820
For further details of day time services between E. Lancs and London refer to service 910

Illustration 2: The post deregulation inter-city coach service

NATIONAL EXPRESS »

Table 247 Table 247

487 **Nottingham** – LEICESTER – NORTHAMPTON – OXFORD – READING – WINCHESTER – SOUTHAMPTON – **Portsmouth**   487

Showing connections with Service 460

Valid from 21 September 1980 to 16 May 1981 inclusive

For Bank Holiday arrangements see below	487
Days of operation	D
NOTTINGHAM. Victoria Bus Stn	0850
Nottingham University, Highfields, Bus Lay-by	0900
Beeston. Bus Stn	0905
Long Eaton. Green	0913
Kegworth. P.O.	0927
Hathern. Green	0931
Loughborough. Bus Stn	0940
Quorn. opp. Royal Oak	0946
Mountsorrel. opp. Allen's Garage	0950
Birstall. Sibsons Rd	0957
LEICESTER. St Margarets Bus Stn	1010
Leicester. Bus Bay. London/Evington Rd	1015
Leicester. nr. Grenfell Rd., Stoneygate	1019
Oadby. Ferrolene House	1022
Great Glen. The Greyhound	1026
Kibworth. Rose & Crown Hotel	1030
Market Harborough. Bus Stn	1040
Great Oxendon. Cross Roads	1044
Kelmarsh. Bus Bay	1047
Maidwell. opp. Stag's Head	1050
Lamport. Bus Bay	1054
Brixworth. opp. 97 Northampton Rd	1057
Pitsford Turn	1100
opp. Whitehills Hotel	1102
Kingsthorpe. Swift Electrics	1105
KING'S LYNN. Vancouver Centre Bus Stn	0805A
Wisbech. Horsefair	0830A
PETERBOROUGH. Bishops Rd. Bus Stn	0910A
Market Deeping. Cross Roads	0927A
STAMFORD. Bus Stn	0942A
CORBY. Bus Stn	1015A
Kettering. Bus Stn	1032A
Wellingborough. Commercial Way	1049A
NORTHAMPTON. Greyfriars Bus Stn arr	1115R
NORTHAMPTON. Greyfriars Bus Stn dep	1130
Towcester. Central Garage	1150
Brackley. Market Place	1205
Bicester. Bus Lay-by. Sheep St	1225
OXFORD. Gloucester Green Coach Stn arr	1250R
OXFORD. Gloucester Green Coach Stn dep	1305
Dorchester. High St	1320
Wallingford. Town Hall	1330
Streatley. Bull Hotel	1340
Pangbourne. George Hotel. The Square	1350
READING. Bus Stn	1405
Basingstoke. Bus Stn	1440
WINCHESTER. Worthy Lane Coach Stn arr	1510R
WINCHESTER. Worthy Lane Coach Stn dep	1540
Eastleigh. Stand A. Upper Market St	1555
Southampton Airport +	1558
SOUTHAMPTON. Bedford Place Coach Stn arr	1610
SOUTHAMPTON. Bedford Place Coach Stn dep	1610
SOUTHAMPTON. Royal Pier	1615
Fareham. Bus Stn	1640
Portchester. Newtown Coach Stop	1648
Hilsea. Southdown Coach Stn	1655
North End. London Rd. Kirby Rd	1700
Portsmouth. Mile End Rd. (for Continental Ferry Term	1705
Portsmouth Harbour. The Hard	1710
Southsea. 249 Albert Rd	1715
Southsea. South Parade. The Dell	1718
Southsea. Clarence Pier. Bus Stands	1720
PORTSMOUTH. Winston Churchill Ave. Coach Stn	1725

For Bank Holiday arrangements see below	487
Days of operation	D
PORTSMOUTH. Winston Churchill Ave. Coach Stn	1115
Southsea. Clarence Pier. Bus Stands	1120
Southsea. South Parade. The Dell	1123
Southsea. 249 Albert Rd	1125
Portsmouth Harbour. The Hard	1130
Portsmouth. Mile End Rd. (for Continental Ferry Term	1135
North End. Gladys Ave. Bus Garage	1140
Hilsea. Lay-by opp. Coach Stn	1145
Portchester. Newtown Coach Stop	1152
Fareham. Bus Stn	1200
SOUTHAMPTON. Royal Pier	1225
SOUTHAMPTON. Bedford Place Coach Stn arr	1230
SOUTHAMPTON. Bedford Place Coach Stn dep	1235
Southampton Airport +	1247
Eastleigh. Stand A. Upper Market St	1250
WINCHESTER. Worthy Lane Coach Stn arr	1305R
WINCHESTER. Worthy Lane Coach Stn dep	1335
Basingstoke. Bus Stn	1405
READING. Bus Stn	1440
Pangbourne. Bus Stop. Station Rd	1455
Streatley. Bull Hotel	1505
Wallingford. Town Hall	1515
Dorchester. High St	1525
OXFORD. Gloucester Green Coach Stn arr	1540
OXFORD. Gloucester Green Coach Stn dep	1545
Bicester. Bus Lay-by. Sheep St	1615
Brackley. Market Place	1635
Towcester. Central Garage	1650
NORTHAMPTON. Greyfriars Bus Stn arr	1710R
NORTHAMPTON. Greyfriars Bus Stn dep	1730
Wellingborough. Commercial Way	1825A
Kettering. Bus Stn	1840A
CORBY. Bus Stn	1857A
STAMFORD. Bus Stn	1927A
Market Deeping. Cross Roads	1940A
PETERBOROUGH. Bishops Rd. Bus Stn	1955A
Wisbech. Horsefair	2027A
KING'S LYNN. Vancouver Centre Bus Stn	2050A
Kingsthorpe. Cock Hotel	1735
Whitehills Hotel	1738
Pitsford Turn	1740
Brixworth. 101 Northampton Rd	1743
Lamport. Swan	1746
Maidwell. Stag's Head	1750
Kelmarsh. Bus Bay	1753
Great Oxendon. Cross Roads	1756
Market Harborough. Bus Stn	1800
Kibworth. opp. Rose & Crown Hotel	1810
Great Glen. The Greyhound	1814
Oadby. opp. Ferrolene House	1818
Leicester. Shanklin Drive. Stoneygate	1821
Leicester. Bus Bay. Victoria Park Gates	1825
LEICESTER. St Margarets Bus Stn	1835
Birstall. opp. Sibsons Rd	1847
Mountsorrel. Dog & Gun	1853
Quorn. Royal Oak	1857
Loughborough. Bus Stn	1905
Hathern. Green	1914
Kegworth. P.O.	1918
Long Eaton. Green	1932
Beeston. Bus Stn	1940
Nottingham University. Highfields. Bus Lay-by	1945
NOTTINGHAM. Victoria Bus Stn	1955

COACHMASTERS ARE VALID ON THESE SERVICES

CODE   **A**   Service 460. Passengers will be required to change coaches at Northampton

BANK HOLIDAY ARRANGEMENTS
Christmas 25, 26 December 1980 No service
Normal service will operate on all other dates

For explanation of standard notes see introduction

NATIONAL EXPRESS »

| **487** | **Lincoln** – NEWARK – NOTTINGHAM – LEICESTER – NORTHAMPTON – OXFORD – READING – WINCHESTER – SOUTHAMPTON – **Portsmouth** | **487** |

Showing connections with Service 721

For Bank Holiday arrangemens see below	487	721
Days of operation	D	D
LINCOLN, St. Marks Bus Stn	0755	...
North Hykeham, Cross Roads	0805	...
NEWARK, Bus Stn	0825	...
NOTTINGHAM, Victoria Bus Stn	0900	...
LEICESTER, St. Margarets Bus Stn., Platform 12	0945	...
NORTHAMPTON, Greyfriars Bus Stn. arr.	1040R	...
NORTHAMPTON, Greyfriars Bus Stn. dep.	1100	...
Towcester, Central Garage	1120	...
Brackley, Market Place	1135	...
Bicester, Bus Lay-by, Sheep St	1155	...
OXFORD, Gloucester Green Coach Stn. arr.	1220R	...
OXFORD, Gloucester Green Coach Stn dep.	1240	...
READING, Bus Stn	1335	...
Basingstoke, Bus Stn	1410	...
WINCHESTER, Bus Stn., Broadway arr.	1440R	...
WINCHESTER, Bus Stn., Broadway dep.	1500	...
Eastleigh, Stand A, Upper Market St	1520	...
SOUTHAMPTON, Bedford Place Coach Stn arr.	1535	⇨
SOUTHAMPTON, Bedford Place Coach Stn dep.	1535	1550
SOUTHAMPTON, Royal Pier, Museum	1540	
Fareham, Bus Stn	1605	
Portsmouth, Mile End Rd. (for Continental Ferry Term.)	1625	
PORTSMOUTH, The Hard Interchange, Bay A	1630	
HILSEA, Bus Garage	1645	
BOURNEMOUTH, Coach Stn	...	1650

For Bank Holiday arrangements see below	721	487
Days of operation	D	D
BOURNEMOUTH, Coach Stn	1110	...
HILSEA, Bus Garage		1140
PORTSMOUTH, The Hard Interchange, Bay B		1155
Portsmouth, Mile End Rd. (for Continental Ferry Term.)		1200
Fareham, Bus Stn		1220
SOUTHAMPTON, Royal Pier, by Main Gate opp. Museum		1245
SOUTHAMPTON, Bedford Place Coach Stn arr.	1210	1250
SOUTHAMPTON, Bedford Place Coach Stn dep.	⇦	1255
Eastleigh, Stand A, Upper Market St	...	1310
WINCHESTER, Bus Stn., Broadway arr.	...	1330R
WINCHESTER, Bus Stn., Broadway dep.	...	1350
Basingstoke, Bus Stn	...	1420
READING, Bus Stn	...	1455
OXFORD, Gloucester Green Coach Stn. arr.	...	1550R
OXFORD, Gloucester Green Coach Stn. dep.	...	1610
Bicester, Bus Lay-by, Sheep St	...	1635
Brackley, Market Place	...	1655
Towcester, Central Garage	...	1710
NORTHAMPTON, Greyfriars Bus Stn. arr.	...	1730R
NORTHAMPTON, Greyfriars Bus Stn. dep.	...	1745
LEICESTER, St. Margarets Bus Stn., Platform 12	...	1840
NOTTINGHAM, Victoria Bus Stn	...	1925
NEWARK, Bus Stn	...	2025
North Hykeham, Cross Roads	...	2045
LINCOLN, St. Marks Bus Stn	...	2055

Opposite:

Illustration 3: A typical National Express cross country service in 1980

Above:

Illustration 4: By 1983, the service had evolved to this

2.2.5 THE BRITISH RAIL RESPONSE

The threat posed by deregulation was recognised at the outset by British Rail. Their response throughout the period has been evolutionary rather than revolutionary. Table 5 catalogues the main initiatives which have been launched since October 1980 and were, at least primarily, prompted by coach competition. The majority of these initiatives fall under two categories. The first is the railcard. This was by no means a new concept, having been available to senior citizens, students and families for some years previously. Family railcards, however, were reduced in price by 33% with greater flexibility allowed in the definition of the eligible group. The student railcard was extended to all persons under 24 years of age. The philosophy is abundantly clear. Sectors of the market which are most price sensitive (the young, the elderly, the group) are offered cheap travel in order to dissuade them from seeking alternative modes of transport. Moreover, although its effect has never been fully researched to our knowledge, the requirement to initially purchase the card is a subtle way of increasing modal loyalty - the more one travels the more one saves.

British Rail's key response to coach competition has been the Supersave, later renamed Inter-City saver ticket. These fares (return tickets available at off peak times when spare capacity exists) were first tested on journeys between Liverpool and London. The £9 return fare represented a saving of over 50% on the existing *day* return rail fare. It was also highly competitive with the then new £8 low coach fare. The results were dramatic and the scheme was quickly extended to other routes. Table 6 shows why.

Virtually all main flows on the Inter-City network are now covered by saver fares. Although the relative price of such bargain offers has not remained at such a low level, this can clearly be considered as a major and, for the immediate future at least, enduring response to cheap coach fares.

Two important points should be made concerning saver fares. Attention should be paid to the sequence of introduction in Table 5. This reveals that the prime focus was upon those routes and journeys where competition was most severe. Hence Liverpool was followed

Table 5
Selected Catalogue of British Rail Initiatives since the Act

October 1980	Family Railcard reduced to £10. Under 24's Railcard introduced
November 1980	Persons with Senior Citizens Railcard offered £1 to anywhere day returns
January 1981	Introduction of Liverpool to London Supersave ticket
May/June 1981	Supersaves extended to West Midlands and Manchester to London routes; also on Inter City 125 routes between West of England and London
August 1981	Saver fares extended to all London Midland Region principal stations
October 1981	Extension of 'Grocery Voucher' Scheme
January 1982	Saver fares become nationwide
May 1982	Introduction of Nightrider: low fare all 1st class train with catering, running overnight London-Edinburgh-Glasgow and vice versa.
October 1982/ May 1983	Redeployment of Inter City 125 trains to include East Midlands/Sheffield-London route, giving more cost effective use of high quality trains
Late 1983	Progressive extension of Saver fares for cross country Inter City journeys, but changes in pricing policy, including the introduction of higher fare for outward travel on Fridays

by the West Midlands, the West of England, etc. Journeys *from* London were not necessarily introduced at the same time. Where this was so, the fare was in some cases higher than if the journey had commenced in the provinces. Furthermore, it is instructive to consider the nature of the routes initially selected. There is a clear correlation between these routes and the quality of service offered. The better the service, the earlier the cheap fares were offered.

The second point concerns the question of whether such schemes are cost effective. This has certainly been a matter of contention amongst coach operators and indeed the whole policy of cheap fares was called into question by the Serpell Committee (1983). British Rail data, however, suggests that the policy of cutting fares is not at the expense of the taxpayer. This claim is made on the basis that the long run marginal costs of rail operations are extremely low (Table 7). A fascinating comparison of marginal cost is illustrated in Table 8. Note that this is expressed in terms of cost per seat mile. The critical test is the capability of rail to exploit its higher carrying capacity. Coach competition is, in itself, a major threat to the achievement of such a goal.

Table 6

Volume and Revenue Benefits of London Savers (September 1981)

	Liverpool-London	Manchester-London	Birmingham-London
Growth in volume	+116%	+92%	+64%
Growth in revenue	+ 22%	+10%	+14%

Source: Bleasdale (1983 b.)

Table 7
Additional Costs and Revenue per Passenger Mile:
Liverpool - London Saver

Pence per mile at 1983 prices	1981 Scheme	1983 Scheme
Additional cost per passenger mile	0.9	0.7
Additional revenue per passenger mile	0.9	0.8

Source: Bleasdale (1983 b.)

Table 8
Coach and Rail : Comparison of Costs

Marginal cost per seat mile	Pence per seat mile
Assuming 400 miles per day of:	
45 seat road coach	1.5
57 seat road coach	1.4
Electric Inter-City train	1.2
Diesel High Speed Train	1.7
Extra 72 seat rail coach	0.5
Assuming 800 miles per day of:	
Electric Inter-City train	0.9
Diesel High Speed Train	1.3
Extra 72 seat rail coach	0.4

Source: Bleasdale (1983 b.)

These findings are significant to any discussion of the merits of coach and rail competition. Our purpose here is simply to relate the effects of deregulation and we must therefore return to the consequences of competition and the response of British Rail. To synthesize, despite the success of the above initiatives, British Rail have suffered as a result of deregulation. Bleasdale (1983a) estimates losses in relation to the Inter-City network of approximately £12 million in 1981, rising to £15 million in 1982. This should be set against a turnover of some £450 million.

These calculations are based upon British Rail's own market research, which suggests that 30% of new coach travellers would otherwise have travelled by rail. This is broadly in line with our own findings and does not seem anomalous with the surveys of upmarket coaches (discussed in Section 2.2.2) which revealed a predictably higher transfer of 40-55%. The British Rail share of the combined inter-city coach and rail market appears to have slipped from around 90 to 80%, although in some cases, as in Oxford (illustrated in Table 9) and the East Midlands (Section 3.3.3), the situation has deteriorated to a somewhat greater extent.

Table 9

Estimated Rail Percentage Share of Rail/Scheduled Coach Market

	Nov 1980	Jan 1981	June 1981	Nov 1981	June 1982
London to:					
Oxford	75	60	64	60	52
South Wales	90	84	79	87	81
Bristol/West of England	90	78	72	87	80
Bristol	n a	n a	63	80	71
West of England	n a	n a	77	91	84

Source: Bleasdale (1983 a.)

2.3 EXCURSIONS AND TOURS

At the outset, we must state that even the most cursory review of the excursions and tours sector is a difficult task. The fragmentary nature of the market and its commercial competitiveness (even before deregulation) make it very difficult to reach firm conclusions. The comments below are therefore offered as a general review of the total market, with an emphasis upon significant developments which have gained publicity.

Given the above, it is perhaps most appropriate to begin with national statistics. The changed definitions under the 1980 Act do not assist us here. The figures for 1980 shown in Table 10 include a number of services which are no longer categorised as excursions and tours. Taking this into consideration, there is an apparent upturn in the market in the first two years following deregulation, although growth was not maintained during 1983. An editorial in Coaching Journal (December 1983) described the year as non-vintage.

A lot of small operators of considerable stature went out of business. How much this was caused by over enthusiastic expansion, how much by the acquisition of too much expensive metal - usually of foreign manufacture - and how much as a result of the recession is hard to say. But it was a fact that costs escalated and traffic fell.

Table 10
Passenger Journeys : Excursions and Tours Operations

	1980	1981	1982	1983
Provision by:				
Independent operators	18	17	26	26
National Bus Company	6	6	6	5
Other public sector operators	1	1	2	2
Total (millions)	25	24	34	33

Note: Changed definitions. Figures for 1980 include operations subsequently reclassified as stage carriage.

Source: Adapted from Department of Transport

Some care is needed in seeking to derive any trend from these results. Whilst the market, in common with express, had been in decline since the mid 1970s, annual changes have traditionally been more volatile. 1979 for instance had shown a 10% growth on 1978, whereas 1980 was particularly poor. Whatever the long term uncertainty, the last three years have witnessed significant change in this sector. Whilst deregulation itself has been a considerable stimulus, one might suggest that other factors have played an equally important role.

Wilson (1982) went so far as to describe deregulation as a 'damp squib'. He cited the fact that licences for excursions and tours had become extremely easy to acquire and that changes in the market for travel were more important. In particular, he declared that public tastes were changing - a factor emphasized by many operators - with increases in the demand for the more personalised services which coach travel can provide. A further effect had been the influence of the wide range of new luxury vehicles on the market. Without question, there was a growing belief that competition was not simply about price. It also concerned quality.

The combination of all these factors has been leading to significant changes within the market. Operators are starting to become increasingly specialised in relation to the services which they provide. Underlying this is a shift away from the traditional seaside excursion and British tour, to special events, long distance day trips and continental holidays. This is well illustrated by the growth of coach traffic at Dover Harbour, shown in Table 11. In passenger terms, such growth meant that appproximately 4.6 million persons crossed the channel by coach in 1983, compared to 4.3 million in private cars. Note that this period of expansion has taken place both before and after deregulation. A consequence of the growth has been the investment of £7.8 million by the Harbour Board in a new coach terminal to accommodate such an increase.

Changing markets and the freedom of deregulation have inevitably led many operators to view the 1980 Act as something of a mixed blessing. Carnell (1983), a Sheffield based operator, illustrates this in his article 'Commitment to Quality'. He declares himself still in favour of deregulation, since it enabled the operator to give the public what *they* wanted. Subsequently, he severely criticises the way that several operators have acted in offering unrealistically cheap services.

> Many operators just did not know what it cost to operate coaches in present day conditions.

Rather paradoxically, he also goes on to call for the licensing (regulation?) of tour organisers.

The view that there is potential for profit in some aspects of this sector is clearly borne out by a growing interest from both municipal and passenger transport executive operators. The development of this role by Leicester City Transport is documented elsewhere in this report. Articles in the technical press suggest that this is by no means an isolated example. Indeed, considerable disquiet has been provoked amongst some independent operators. Keen (1983), suggests that the continuing entry of municipal operators into contract, private hire and excursions poses a very serious threat to the future financial well being of the small operator.

Table 11
Coach Traffic at Dover

Year	Number of Coaches	Annual Growth	
		Absolute	Percentage
1977	33,457	--	--
1978	39,807	+ 6,350	19.0
1979	49,182	+ 9,375	23.6
1980	62,473	+ 13,291	27.0
1981	87,037	+ 24,564	39.3
1982	110,743	+ 23,705	27.2

Source: Dover Harbour Board

2.4 QUALITY CONTROL ASPECTS

Deregulation related to the removal of quantity controls. Just as in similar situations relating to both shipping and civil aviation, it was perhaps inevitable that certain aspects of quality control arising from this action would also come to the fore. The authors have attended several discussions on deregulation where issues of safety, such as speeding, tachographs, and drivers' hours have been paramount issues. It would therefore seem inappropriate to conclude without a brief discussion on two major issues of public concern.

One of the major problems faced by operators entering or expanding into the express and excursions and tours markets has been lack of infrastructure. This has applied particularly in London due to both the National Bus Company's ownership (and hence exclusive use) of the major coach station, and the emphasis upon the capital as a destination for new express services. Sir Kenneth Newman (1983), the Metropolitan Police Commissioner, has criticised coach deregulation as a consequence. He argued,

> The recent relaxation in the legislation relating to coach operation has created many difficulties for the police. Operators are able to choose terminals, routes and picking up points without the police having any opportunity to make representations.

The main black spots were stated to be around Victoria Coach Station and King's Cross. Streets around the stations were used by non-licensed operators and police were 'holding the ring' between competing operators. Numerous complaints of obstruction had been made between rival companies. The continuing expansion of commuter coaches is not serving to alleviate this concern.

An even greater issue arose during 1983. An unfortunate coincidence of several road accidents involving coaches on motorways generated a considerable amount of media publicity. The question of whether coaches should be allowed to travel at 70 mph on motorways, along with the additional question of alleged violation of this limit, became regular debating points. The Government deflected much of this concern by announcing that it would carry out checks regarding the allegations of speeding. No formal report on these findings has been produced, although it has been stated that the incidence of speeding was by no means as widespread as believed. How much this is bound up with the major publicity campaign launched by the Bus and Coach Council to alert its members to the dangers of speeding (and the surveys!), followed by its adoption of a voluntary code of conduct in relation to this issue, remains conjecture.

However, in February 1984, Mrs. Lynda Chalker, the Transport Minister, announced that permitted coach speeds on dual carriageways would be raised to 60 mph so as to more logically conform with speeds on single carriageway roads (50 mph) and motorways (70 mph). At least in relative terms, coaching has been declared to be safe.

REFERENCES

Barton, A.J. and Everest, J.T. (1984). *Express Coach Services in the three years following the 1980 Transport Act.* Transport and Road Research Laboratory Report 1127.

Birks, J. (1983). *The effects of deregulation on National Express.* PTRC Summer Meeting, Volume L.

Bleasdale, C. (1983a). *The effects of deregulation on Inter-City Rail Services.* PTRC Summer Meeting, Volume L.

Bleasdale, C. (1983b). *Transport & Mobility.* Paper to Chartered Institute of Transport meeting, London, 14 November.

Carnell, T. (1983). *Commitment to Quality.* Coaching Journal, September.

Department of Transport (1981/82/83/84). *Transport Statistics Great Britain (Annual publication).* HMSO.

Dodds, N. (1983). *Fewer chances for newcomers.* Motor Transport, 2 March.

Fairhead, R.D., Jackson, R.L. and Watts, P.F. (1983). *Developments in long distance commuter coaching following the Transport Act 1980.* Transport and Road Research Laboratory Report 1038.

Gorman, B. (1982). *Deregulation of Express Services.* Paper to BCC/UTSG Joint Seminar, Manchester, December.

Keen, D. (1983). Quoted in *Municipal competition 'could mean end of small operator'*. Motor Transport, 3 August.

Kent, A. (1984). *The role of independent 'up market' trunk coach services*. Coaching Journal, February.

MacBriar, I.D. (1982). *NBC's response to the 1980 Transport Act*. Transport Economists Group Newsletter, No.1.

National Bus Company (1984). *Annual Report 1983*.

Newman, Sir K. (1983). Quoted in Commercial Motor, 29 October.

Serpell Report (1983). *Railway Finances*. HMSO.

White, P.R. (1983a). *Express coach services in Britain since Deregulation*. PTRC Summer Meeting July 1983, Volume M.

White, P.R. (1983b). *How far can commuter coaching grow?* Coaching Journal, December 1983.

White, P.R. (1984) *Commuter coaches - threat or asset?*. Transport Economist, Number 2.

Whittle, R. (1983) *Spend at least 20% of your time on paperwork*. Motor Transport, 16 March.

Wilson, J. (1982). *Deregulation of express services*. Paper to BCC/UTSG Joint Seminar, Manchester, December 1982.

SECTION 3. THE EAST MIDLANDS

3.1 INTRODUCTION

We present here the results of our detailed research into the events in the region. The East Midlands contains just over 2 million inhabitants (standard region definition). It comprises a mix of urban concentrations and extensive rural hinterlands. As explained in Section 1.2, it was selected in the expectation of providing a suitable proxy for the country as a whole. Comparison with nationwide events suggests that this has been the case. Whatever the validity of this assertion, we emphasize that particular attention has been given to constructing survey samples which offer an adequate representation of the distribution of coaching activities throughout this region.

There are three main sections. In the first, the actions and attitudes of the large number of firms which make up the independent sector, along with the views of publicly owned companies, are presented. This gives a good catalogue of the industry's general reactions to the Act. The context in which actions and reactions have taken place is also established. There is a particular emphasis upon attitudinal aspects, for example: the perception of opportunity; the nature of competition; the way in which views may have changed over time.

Sections 3.3 and 3.4 relate the factual evidence of changes in express and excursions and tours services respectively. Within the former, we are able to present a detailed analysis of developments in service provision. Inevitably, the performance of National Express is the subject of particular scrutiny. Unfortunately, the lack of adequate data sources make it impossible to analyse the excursions and tours market in such depth. We are, however, able to present results from coach user surveys relating to both types of operation. A good selection of operators, both public and private sector, and range of service provision are included.

39

3.2 VIEWS AND REACTIONS OF THE INDUSTRY

3.2.1 INDEPENDENT OPERATOR SURVEY (1981)

Prior to the legislation, information relating to the services provided by an operator could be derived from the records of the Traffic Commissioners. The regulatory system required a route licence to be held for all express services, excursions and tours. There were limitations to the value of this data. It is well known that operators often held some licences which they did not regularly operate. In terms of adequacy of records, this deficiency pales into insignificance after 1980. Although there is a duty to notify the Commissioners of new and amended express services (see Section 3.3.2.) along with subsequent modifications and withdrawals, the latter aspects in particular have often been ignored in practice. No such obligation to notify is required for excursions and tours. Information on these services is only available from local publicity, or directly from the operator.

A decision was therefore taken to make a direct approach to as many firms as possible, in order to gain a clear indication of new, modified or withdrawn services. Information was also sought on the operator's general perception of the Act. In order to ensure an adequate quantity of respondents, independent operators were sent a short questionnaire. The names and addresses were obtained from the Little Red Book (see Table 2 for an analysis of the size and location of the companies). The results of this survey are presented below. Detailed discussions with a sample of these firms, along with some larger public sector operators, are contained in the next section.

The survey took place at the end of 1981. Operators were therefore canvassed just over one year after the legislation was enacted. Their views on deregulation may have been influenced accordingly. Some possible effects are listed below :

   i Operators would have had time to adjust to the new operating conditions which they faced and their original opinions of the legislation confirmed or disproven.

   ii Some interaction would have taken place between operators, and some opinions formed as a consequence, in addition to those gained from direct observation or experience.

   iii Firms which had ceased trading, or in some cases, had formed mergers were unlikely to respond to the questionnaire.

It was not possible to establish all of the firms falling into these categories, although we received around 10 returns which indicated a direct influence by at least one of these effects.

A total of 60 completed forms were returned, representing over 35% of the Red Book total. This was considered satisfactory, especially since a reasonable cross section of firms, both geographically and in terms of fleet size, were represented. If anything, a small bias occurred towards the larger operator. Bearing this in mind, it can be hypothesized that non-responses might comprise firms which did not consider the legislation worthy of comment. A copy of the questionnaire appears in Appendix A.

Table 12 relates to the size and characteristics of the firms. This provides further evidence of the small scale nature of most independent operators discussed in Section 1.3. For example, 50% of firms are shown to employ not more than 10 persons (full and part-time). 30% of firms do not employ full time staff on vehicle maintenance, whilst for most of the remainder it was only one person. Similarly, 35% of companies have no full time administrator. The table also reveals the close relationship between the number of coaches owned and the total vehicle fleet. In other words, buses, mini-buses etc., are of little consequence. Although many independents own coaches because of their inherent versatility, this gives a clear indication of the nature of their work.

This is confirmed by Table 13. In absolute terms and on the basis of the ranking system employed in the questionnaire, works and school contracts, along with private hire, show a considerable dominance. The former was identified as the most important aspect of their business by 57% of respondents. The questionnaire was deliberately unspecific in its use of the phrase 'rank by importance'. The uniformity of response, and subsequent discussions, have indicated that most operators made this judgement in relation to the revenue gained from each type of operation.

The table also permits comparison of the immediate pre and post Act situation. The figures do not appear to indicate dramatic change. The number of operators providing express and excursions and tours shows only marginal change, although this should perhaps be compared with an apparent decline in the other named types of service. Even so, consideration of the ranking index (which enables an increase or decrease in the scale of operation within any category to be established) indicates that the changes which have occurred appear limited in an overall context. The relative importance of

Table 12

Independent Operator Survey: Firm Size and Characteristics

1. Characteristics of Firm in relation to:

Size	Number of Vehicles	Number of Coaches	Number of Staff
1- 5	21	23	7
6-10	19	21	23
11-20	12	12	14
21-50	8	4	5
50+	0	0	11

2. Relationship between Coach and Total Vehicle Ownership

Number of Vehicles	Number of Coaches			
	1-5	6-10	11-20	21-50
1- 5	19			
6-10	3	18		
11-20	1	3	8	
21-50	0	0	4	4

3. Categorisation of Firms by Staff Employment

Persons in each category	Drivers		Conductors		Maintenance		Administration	
	Full Time	Part Time	Full Time	Part Time	Full Time	Part Time	Full Time	Part Time
0	9	17	56	54	18	48	21	41
1- 5	29	26	4	5	41	12	35	19
6-10	12	9	0	1	1	0	3	0
11-20	10	5	0	0	0	0	1	0
21-50	0	2	0	0	0	0	1	0
50+	0	1	0	0	0	0	0	0

Note: n = 60

Table 13

Independent Operator Survey: Types of Service Before and After the Act

	Percentage of Operators Providing Services		Overall Importance Index Based on Ranking *	
	Pre Act	*Post Act*	*Pre Act*	*Post Act*
Stage Carriage	36	31	81	56
Express	34	34	45	49
Excursions and Tours	59	65	116	118
School/Works Contract	91	79	240	207
Private Hire	88	78	227	182

* Operators ranked importance of service 1-5. Index based
on 1st importance = 5; 2nd = 4 etc.; No Provision = 0 points.
Highest score therefore means most important.

Table 14

Independent Operator Survey: Changes in Service Provision
(Figures in percentages)

	Express Services		Excursions and Tours		
Action/Response	*Change in service provision*	*Effects due to the Act*	*Change in service provision*	*Effects due to the Act*	*Other change to business due to Act*
No change/no effect	68	67	50	47	33
Provided new or increased services/ positive	13	13	32	30	38
Withdrawn or reduced services/negative	7	7	12	15	14
No response	12	12	5	7	8
Other response (not related to service provision)	n a	n a	n a	n a	8

different service categories has not changed in this period, whilst only 9% of firms altered *any* of their scorings of 'order of importance' in relation to the five types of service listed.

More detailed changes relating to express and excursions and tours were identifiable from the responses to questions 6 to 9 of the survey (Appendix A). These were deliberately open ended and brought forth several useful comments as summarised below. Quantification of the responses has necessitated some generalisation. However, we believe that our adoption of a simple positive/negative/neutral categorisation still permits an accurate picture of action and response to be presented. The relevant statistics are shown in Table 14.

Using this system of classification, our view is that deregulation has provided a stimulus, albeit to a far greater extent in the excursions and tours sector, and that this has manifested itself in new and increased services more than retrenchment. The correlation between changes in service provision and the stated effect of the Act as a causal factor is self evident. Whilst we might urge some caution in interpretation, given both the topicality of deregulation and the fact that the questionnaire was focussing directly upon the issue, this finding can hardly be dismissed. It does, however, raise the question of cause and effect. Did the attitude of an operator to the Act prompt action, or did the freedom to innovate and the experience subsequently gained help to form opinions of the legislation?

Although it is virtually impossible to establish an irrefutable answer, it is worth reporting that 75% of operators introducing an express service offered a positive general view of the Act (question 9), whilst 63% of the firms introducing new excursions and tours were similarly disposed. Conversely, of those reducing or withdrawing from express, 100% had a negative view, along with 83% of those cutting back their excursions and tours programme.

Table 15 shows an analysis of question 9, which stands in some contrast with the *actions* reported in Table 14. The reason is that the majority of those categorised in the latter as 'no change/no response' have a negative view of the legislation. Given the intention of the legislation to stimulate entrepreneurial flair, the findings in Table 15 may be seen as disappointing. At best, it demonstrates a considerable mix in both the nature of coach operation and willingness to take risk within this sector of the industry. Due to the limited sample size, we were unable to satisfactorily establish whether differences occurred between the actions and attitudes of a firm and its fleet size. Positive action in providing new services did, however, appear more likely amongst larger firms. Finally, we endeavour to summarise the comments contained in the free response sections of questions 6 to 9. The views reported are those which were found to occur with greatest frequency.

The main concern of those seeing the Act as a disbenefit was the suggestion that it would bring, or had brought, unprecedented levels of competition, resulting in too many operators chasing too few passengers. This was seen to favour incoming firms at the expense of established businesses. These views appear to be at some odds with subsequent experience, which tends to show that the established operator has the advantage, both in terms of local knowledge, and an awareness of the problems involved in service provision. Examples of this include contact with hoteliers and the optimal location of pick up and set down points. Some operators did point out that increased competition was likely to be temporary in nature, as the market would eventually exclude 'the cowboys'.

The increase in competition was considered to necessitate a wider area of pick up points in the search for more passengers. Other adverse comments to the new legislation included the feeling that it was too late, being directed towards an industry already suffering the consequences of high unemployment and falling custom. Reduced loadings, particularly on excursions, were reported by a number of firms. Other aspects of competition received attention, such as 'price war', 'unfair and unethical' and 'a temporary gain to passengers at the expense of operator profits'.

One of the most widely reported advantages of deregulation was the increase in flexibility offered to operators in their choice of

Table 15
Independent Operator Survey: General View of the 1980 Act

Attitude	Percentage of Firms
General indifference / little change	7
Positive benefit to the firm	36
Negative effect on the firm	38
No response	19

destination for excursions and tours. This had led many operators to provide a more varied programme for their summer season, whilst several claimed to be in the process of planning an increase in excursions for the following (1982) season. These comments were especially prevalent amongst operators who did not operate any services prior to the Act or who had a limited and restricted number of excursions licences. It was also considered possible to provide a more comprehensive service, offering greater choice to the passenger. In this context, it was claimed that whilst the Act had not necessarily been without disadvantages, it also provided a greater potential for profit, along with better loadings. The wider pick up area question was seen by some as an advantage in offering the opportunity to seek new markets and, hence, attract more passengers. The change in the definition of express had also brought an unexpected benefit to some operators. This was where some works services had been licensed as express under the pre 1980 definition. Conversion, in certain circumstances, to a stage carriage licence had allowed fuel duty rebate to be claimed.

The advantages expressed above can be summed up by the one comment, 'we can go where we like, when we like'. Certainly, some operators were unreserved in their praise of the new legislation as 'a tremendous asset.... encouraging more use of coach travel'.

3.2.2 INTERVIEWS WITH OPERATORS

To gain a more detailed impression of the effects of deregulation on the independent sector and to establish views within the public sector, a series of interviews were held during the first year of the research period. Fourteen independent firms of varying size, located throughout the region are represented. These are listed in Appendix B. Although the selection process was not rigorous in a statistical sense, care was taken to ensure a cross section of viewpoints arising from the original questionnaire. Seven operators, known to have launched new express and/or excursions and tours since the Act, were included, whilst the remainder had stated themselves to be either indifferent to (and unaffected by) the legislation, or in the process of reducing their services. This produces an intentional bias towards those firms which had embarked upon service innovations since the Act. The public sector operators include four local subsidiary companies of the National Bus Company. Although several meetings were held with National Express, the views of the operator are felt to be adequately represented elsewhere in the report and do not require repetition here (see also Birks J. reference at the end of Section 2). We also include brief comments with regard to Leicester City Transport. This is the only municipal undertaking in our study area which appears to have made a major response to deregulation in the areas of express and excursions and tours.

Independent Operators with fleets between 15 and 260 vehicles
Seven firms are represented here, including (disproportionately) four who had launched regular frequency express services to London.

i Express
The Act provided an opportunity to consider innovations in the express market which, in some cases, had been desired (by the firm) for some time. It gave one operator a chance to utilise excess vehicle capacity. No firm reported evidence of carrying out market research before starting a new service, although one operator had run an excursion on the same route as the subsequent express service. This was deemed a useful way of testing the potential market. Nevertheless, the decision to select a particular route was justified by all operators as 'the obvious choice'. In all cases, the destination was London. Given this, it is important to record that none of the interviewees declared any plans, or even desires, for further innovation. General attitudes to express confirm the questionnaire survey with a range of views from 'a useful part of the business' and 'a definite method of advertising the company name outside the immediate locality' to 'of no particular significance'.

The principal problem mentioned in operating express was traffic congestion in London. Other difficulties included arranging satisfactory pick up and set down points, refreshment stops, the effects of recession and 'unfair competition' from other operators. The main service origin for all operators was their local town base.

Operators providing express did not appear to have a very thorough grasp of passenger characteristics. Most suggested that the majority of passengers had been attracted from cars (compare survey results, Section 3.3.4), although one operator cited newly generated travel. No particular age group of traveller was identified, although students were defined as important users. There was a similar lack of knowledge in relation to passenger journey purpose.

ii Excursions and Tours
With the exception of one operator, all respondents considered that the excursion market was changing, with a shift away from the traditional seaside destination towards the special event; for example, pop concerts. Similarly, most also believed that passenger

numbers were increasing. The longer distance excursion was becoming more popular, with the motorway programme having made this possible. This trend was thought to have been in evidence before the Act. The legislation provided a catalyst in this respect rather than the major innovation. The great advantage of deregulation was agreed by all to be its flexibility. The opportunity to plan and experiment with programmes without licensing restriction was a considerable benefit.

The situation in the tours market received a more varied response. Three operators showed great enthusiasm, particularly in relation to continental holiday work. The remainder expressed a mixture of indifference and pessimism.

iii General

Views on advertising were mixed, ranging from 'a vastly increased budget' to 'nothing has changed'. The need to market the product was, nonetheless, accepted by most firms as an increasing necessity. This was deemed directly attributable to the extra competitiveness brought about by the Act. Keeping the company name in the public eye was vital. As a consequence, two operators had joined an organisation which pooled resources for publicity on excursions and tours, leading to a higher quality travel brochure.

Administration was stated to have been reduced, although some felt that the increasing complexity of drivers' hours and European Community (EEC) regulations were substantially offsetting the gains of delicensing. Another external factor was the effect of recession. It was often mentioned that this, in itself, was bringing about greater competition in coaching.

Provision of coach services was felt to be much easier following deregulation, although one respondent did complain of an increase in costs due to the tightening of quality controls under the 1980 Act, namely operator licensing and the annual vehicle examination. At the same time, this was seen to be of some benefit, since it would remove certain 'cowboys' from the industry.

Finally, the effect of deregulation on the potential for profit. Responses varied more here than on any other issue. The full spectrum of views from a significant increase or decrease in both the short and/or long term were encountered.

Independent Operators with Fleets below 15 Vehicles

Seven firms comprise this sample, only one of whom had been involved in seasonal express before the 1980 Act. All had some experience of excursions and/or tours.

i Express

Deregulation had produced little change in this area. It is not an exaggeration to describe the general attitude as one of almost total lack of interest. The reasons for this included: 'the firm is too small'; 'the ridiculously competitive situation'; and, 'the country is already fully covered by other operators' services'. The one firm involved in seasonal express before the Act stated that loadings were getting progressively worse. This was not thought to be a consequence of deregulation, since there had been no increase in competition. Another operator mentioned that competition *was* occuring in his area - particularly the duplication of picking up points. Two firms had decided to try seasonal express work since 1980. The choice of destination was again justified without market research, but as a 'previous idea' which had been frustrated by the licensing laws. The rationale for entering this field was not always associated with total commitment. One reason was, 'solely to position a vehicle for other work', whilst the other firm stated, 'worth a try as an alternative to contract work'.

One firm proved an exception to all of the above. Commencing in the late 1970s, they had deliberately sought to develop a high quality image and were successful in both the private hire and tours field. A decision was made in late 1981 to enter the express market with an executive coach service from Nottingham to London. This vehicle, accommodating a maximum of 24 passengers and offering continental breakfast, toilet, video and radio telephone was a unique development in regular frequency express coaching and has only been paralleled since, to our knowledge, by one operator in North West England. Despite intensive local marketing, the service ceased in late spring 1982. Although public reaction had been extremely favourable, with high levels of patronage during the coincident periods of rail strikes, the operator found that the inflexibility of timings (one return journey each way per day) was inadequate to compete with both National Express and British Rail. If a relaunch were to take place, the operator considered that he would need a minimum frequency of about four journeys per day. Higher capacity vehicles (albeit maintaining luxury standards) were also thought to be more appropriate.

ii Excursions and Tours

Views expressed here conform closely to those of the larger independents. The change in the excursion market was considered to be appreciable. Long distance day trips were taking the place of services of shorter distance and duration. Seaside destinations were in marked decline. Competition was firmly cited as increasing considerably. This was due to both deregulation and the recession, with more operators chasing 'price conscious passengers'. Some degree of specialisation (type of service, vehicle, destination etc.) was considered necessary to meet this challenge.

Passengers were regarded by some operators as now being 'more adventurous'. Their perception of coach travel is thought to be changing, with greater demands for quality of service. Hence, again, the need for specialisation. Nevertheless, the freedom of deregulation, which allows an operator to 'fill in' between contract work with an excursion, was clearly having an impact on the small firms represented here. Despite agreement that many parts of the traditional excursions market were in decline, only one operator expressed outright pessimism with the situation. The greatest potential for expansion related to 'activity orientated events'.

With regard to tours, the one week package was cited as a popular and increasing choice, although some operators felt that the market was highly competitive in terms of price. Beyond certain critical thresholds; for example, £200 for a 14 day tour (1981/82 prices), passenger response was 'unpredictable'. In contrast to the observation on price competition, several operators noted that they did not experience competitive service provision by other operators in their locality.

iii General

Views on advertising were mixed, with some firms reducing their expenditure following poor returns on their newspaper advertisements. Generally, those firms which had entered the market with enthusiasm had marketed their services aggressively.

Overall feelings about the Act were as mixed as the operators survey (Section 3.2.1) had indicated - even amongst this small sample. Some had recognized a very clear relationship between the Act, increased competition, falling prices and declining profits. On the other hand, the potential for profit was seen as 'possibly greater', since firms could readily explore new avenues of business. Others simply felt that deregulation had come too late, with the effects of recession and unemployment making it impossible to generate many new passengers. A further problem was the question of high quality (high cost) vehicles. Although almost all could appreciate that there were potential benefits from such acquisition, the need for a versatile vehicle remained the determining factor in their purchasing behaviour.

Subsidiaries of the National Bus Company

Four of the five National Bus Company territorial operators in the region (East Midlands, Lincolnshire, Trent, United Counties), were interviewed during summer 1982. This was before the transfer of seasonal express services to these companies in the following year. Given that touring activities are the responsibility of National Travel, opinions related to the provision of certain seasonal express services, quasi-express limited stop services and excursions along with each company's role in the vehicle supply and planning for National Express services.

i Express

Seasonal express services were considered to be declining, although not as a consequence of competition which was not emerging as a threat. One note of concern was the view in one company that deregulation had reduced their awareness of the behaviour of competitors. Market research was somewhat greater than amongst independents, though still at a very mundane level, such as monitoring enquiries at booking offices. New routes were generally established by intuition. A policy of 'trial and error' was encouraged by the Act.

The view that the Act allowed greater flexibility in the planning and use of vehicles was recognized in the same manner as the independent sector. One subsidiary in particular had experimented widely with several limited stop services where vehicles would have been otherwise idle, or returning to a garage empty. Although such services were express in nature, they had been licensed as stage carriage (pick up and set down points were less than 30 miles apart). Willingness to innovate in this area was a knock on effect of the 1980 Act, since it was considered that objections from other operators would be far less likely.

ii Excursions

A considerable change in fortunes was reported in this area by three of the subsidiaries. One stated that, 'a fundamental change had occurred'. Having been almost on the point of giving up before the Act, excursions were now regarded as a successful part of the business. The removal of licensing was an important factor in this. The previous system had been 'inhibitive and restrictive'. By contrast, the ability to explore new markets was considered to be of great value. These new markets, in common with the view of independent operators, were long distance day trips and special events - visits to entertainments, hypermarkets etc.. Evening excursions had all but died out (although one operator suggested that this had happened before deregulation).

Views on the total market for excursions, according to the above companies, were that a major increase had taken place. The fourth company, whilst agreeing that specialised excursions had achieved good loadings, viewed the overall demand for services as declining.

iii General

Marketing effort ranged from 'essentially unchanged', to an increase 'in direct response to competition'. One subsidiary declared a move into a more market orientated approach, with a publicity budget related to the level of turnover.

An advantage of the Act, which had not emerged in other discussions, was thought to be the scope for greater co-operation between operators. The ability to avoid the bureaucracy of the Traffic Commissioners was an important factor here. On the other hand, it was considered that a major weakness of the Act was in encouraging operators to attack each other 'with little consideration for entrepreneurial spirit'. Certainly, one operator declared a 'responsive approach' following deregulation, in recognition that the market was continually changing.

A further advantage is that the competitive spirit following deregulation had been helpful at all staff levels, improving both general morale and industrial relations. In overall terms, the view of the Act was at worst neutral and at best positive. It was accepted that the apprehension characterizing the period prior to the enactment was misplaced. There had been a smaller response than expected by independents, and an absence of serious competition. With one exception, the potential for profit was certainly seen to be greater.

Municipal Operators

This type of operator would be unlikely to have figured in a discussion of express and excursions and tours prior to deregulation. Indeed, whilst there have been significant developments by certain operators throughout the country since 1980, the overall picture remains very patchy. Many municipal companies, quite simply, do not own coaches (see Table 1 in Section 1.3 for a guide to East Midlands operators) and have little interest in acquiring any. For these reasons, we did not undertake detailed interviews with municipal operators as part of this research. This appears to have been justified, with the exception of Leicester City Transport. Information on this operator was gained from a lecture by Mr J. Chadwick, then Traffic Superintendent of the company, given to the

Chartered Institute of Transport, East Midlands Section, in November 1982.

Leicester owned a fleet of five coaches at the time of deregulation. They were used entirely for private hire work and were not regarded as a signficant revenue earning part of the business. The Act was seen to offer an opportunity to broaden the base beyond the stage carriage market. It was believed that potential existed for long distance day excursions and tours, both in Britain and on the continent.

Considering the pre deregulation situation of five vehicles and no experience in the market, expansion into coaching had been rapid. Twenty coaches were owned by early 1983 with further growth planned, including the arrival of 'up market' high quality vehicles. The company now operates a wide range of day trips, inclusive British holidays and, from summer 1983, continental tours. It also produces its own travel brochure.

Asked whether such activities were not incompatible or, at least, deflecting the company from its major role as a local bus undertaking, Chadwick did not agree. The 1980 Act had introduced free competition to all. If you didn't fill a gap in the market then others would. Why should they confine themselves to stage carriage? In addition to providing a useful financial return, coaching served to develop the company image within and outside Leicester, and gave a considerable fillip to drivers, providing a relief from local stage carriage operation.

The expansionist views of the undertaking with regard to coaching were further confirmed in mid 1983 when it entered the regular express market. Participating with the Maidstone, and Burnley and Pendle operators, 'the City Flyer' service links Lancashire with Leicester, London and Dover. These companies join Reading and Southend as the only municipal operators with an interest in regular daily express services.

3.2.3 INDEPENDENT OPERATOR SURVEY (1983)

The questionnaire survey of 1981 (Section 3.2.1) had canvassed opinions one year after the introduction of the legislation. It was noted that a strong correlation existed between actions taken and an operator's view of the Act. However, success in a competitive environment is unlikely to be a function of enthusiasm alone. Equally, someone who is not interested in seeking to identify an opportunity in deregulation cannot necessarily expect to remain unaffected by the actions of others. To give some evidence of the outcome of actions indicated in the 1981 survey, it was decided to carry out a small number of telephone interviews. These took place in December 1983. As in the case of the first independent operator survey, a deliberate decision was made to bias the sample towards firms with an interest in either of the two types of service under consideration. All of the operators contacted had, at least since the Act, been involved in excursions and tours. Four firms who had launched year round express services were also included.

Subsequent interpretation must be subject to a recognition of this bias. We are almost certainly giving an over-representation to the level of change within the sector, biassed towards those who initially increased rather than reduced their services. We emphasize that our purpose is to assess the nature of these changes and to present a selection of views from independent operators three years after deregulation. The analysis is presented by type of operation. A full list of companies participating in the survey is given in Appendix C.

Express

The results are summarised in Table 16. A first point to note is the level of consistency between actions in 1981 and 1983. Those who embarked upon a programme of expansion, especially if backed up by a positive attitude to the legislation, remain active. It should be noted, however, that the 1981-83 position of operators who had initially increased their services was generally one of stability rather than further growth. By contrast, those with a negative view of the Act seem to have suffered greatly as a consequence of increased competition. In many respects, this may well indicate that the 1981 view was already conditioned by the early fortunes of the firm and that actions have shaped opinions and not vice versa. This does not hold as true in relation to excursions and tours, discussed below.

The table is divided into three categories of operator. Whilst it can be seen that the independent sector has enjoyed some success in year round operations, the general view is that this has been achieved by careful judgement in selecting just one route and developing it. Certainly, lack of ambition alone suggests that further expansion remains highly improbable. The less happy experience of the fourth operator in this group, who met stiff competition from National Express, is self evident.

Analysis of notifications of new express services (subsequently discussed in Section 3.3.2) indicates that the major intensification of express competition relates to seasonal express. This is borne out by the findings amongst operators classified in category B. One may perceive that the views expressed contain a wide range of indications. Competition, and the approach of the individual operator, varies considerably in this type of market.

Notwithstanding the above, the overall impression confirmed the operators' reported perception of the market in 1981. It is generally recognized that 'things have settled down', with specialisation gradually replacing competition as the watchword. Note also, in this context, the total lack of interest by the sample making up category C. Opportunities for high profit are thought to be slim, and the majority of operators believe that the market is adequately served. Operators who have sustained their services have modified and adapted them to meet the needs of their passengers. They have built upon the experience gained from early practical action and responded to the market. As a final comment on specialisation, two of the three successful year round express operators had little or no involvement in seasonal express before the Act and have not entered this part of the market since.

Excursions and Tours

Trends between 1981-83 in this market have clearly been more variable. Much appears due to a generally accepted view of differences between excursions and tours *per se* (Table 17). Although we emphasize the sampling limitations of our survey, the results (along with other evidence elsewhere in the report) suggest that this is due to *both* types of operation witnessing an increase in supply since deregulation. With regard to many excursions, this stimulus has not generated new demand - rather the market continues to decline. On the other hand, tours have certainly provided an extremely buoyant area in which substantial expansion appears to have reaped financial reward. Operator comment suggests that continental touring has grown particularly quickly (confirming the nationwide picture discussed in Section 2.3).

The position in both the excursions and tours markets has not stabilised in the same way as express. Every indication is that further change and development is inevitable. Several of the operators stressed the need to innovate and experiment, especially in relation to excursions, and to specialise within both types of operation in order to avoid duplication of services. Whether further change will bring additional benefits to the passenger, or whether several operators will discover that they have overreached themselves, remains to be seen.

Table 16
Independent Operator Survey 1983 - Express Services

General View of Deregulation	Express Before Deregulation	Service Provision in 1981	Service Provision and views in 1983	Comparison of services Pre and Post Deregulation
CATEGORY A: New year-round services provided since the Act				
Positive	Seasonal Only	One year round and more seasonal	All services remain. Summer good; winter express is hard to sustain	Increase
Positive	Limited Seasonal	One year round service	Unchanged; no future plans	Increase
Positive	None	One year round service	Increased frequency; patronage up; but no likelihood of other new services	Increase
Negative	Substantial seasonal and some year round	Two new year round services. Pre Act routes unchanged	Discontinued year round services. Unfettered competition from National Express. Act unfair.	Variation
CATEGORY B: Seasonal Express provided before and after the Act				
Positive	Yes	Increase	No change in services. Market buoyant	Increase
Positive	Yes	Increase	No change in services, but passengers declining	Increase
Positive	Yes	Reduction	All withdrawn in 1983 due to competition	Decrease

Table 16
(Continued)

General View of Deregu-lation	Express Before Deregu-lation	Service Provision in 1981	Service Provision and views in 1983	Comparison of services Pre and Post Deregulation
Mixed Blessings	Yes	Unchanged	No discernable change	No change
Indifferent	Yes	Unchanged	No change in services; passengers constant, but more operators in market	No change
Negative	Yes	Unchanged	All withdrawn due to National Bus Company encroachment	Decrease
Negative	Yes	Reduction	All withdrawn 1983 after financial loss in 1982. More coaches in the market - less passengers	Decrease

CATEGORY C: No Express Services before the Act and in 1981

Positive	No	None	(Collective view): None. No likelihood	N/A
Positive	No	None	of becoming involved due to lack of interest and	N/A
Positive	No	None	belief that market is fully or over provided	N/A
Negative	No	None	for.	N/A

Table 17
Independent Operator Survey 1983 - Excursions and Tours

General View of Deregu- lation	Excursions and Tours Before De- regulation	Service Provision in 1981	Service Provision and views in 1983	Comparison of services Pre and Post Deregulation
Positive	Yes	Increase	250% increase on 1981, particularly continental tours	Increase
Positive	Yes	Increase	Good expansion, but constant innovation is important. Market good	Increase
Positive	Yes	Increase	Tours increasing; excursions decreasing	Variation
Positive	Yes	Increase	Tours increasing (continental) but excursions decreasing	Variation
Positive	Yes	Increase	300% increase in tours, but excursion market now highly sensitive. Value for money essential	Variation
Positive	Yes	Increase	New touring destinations, but having to share loads with other operators	Variation
Positive	Yes	Increase	Decreasing. Passengers not forthcoming	Variation
Positive	Yes	Decrease	Remaining constant. Many operators are already in the market	Decrease

Table 17
(Continued)

General View of Deregulation	Excursions and Tours Before Deregulation	Service Provision in 1981	Service Provision and views in 1983	Comparison of services Pre and Post Deregulation
Positive	No	None	Tried day trips, but unsuccessful	Variation
Mixed Blessings	Yes	Increase	Increased service but so have competitors. Future uncertain	Increase
Indifferent	Yes	Increase	Greater variety now offered. Excursions have increased	Increase
Negative	Yes	No change	No change. Competition has increased, but without dramatic effect	No change
Negative	No	No change	Entered market 1982. Tours slightly up during 1983	Increase
Negative	Yes	Decrease	Have increased tours, but seaside excursions reduced	Decrease
Negative	Yes	Decrease	Only limited tours involvement; need to be cautious and selective. Contract work better than excursions	Decrease

3.3 EXPRESS SERVICES

3.3.1. INTRODUCTION AND REVIEW

The review of nationwide events following deregulation explained how attention focussed immediately upon high speed trunk operations to and from London. The East Midlands was no exception. The first few weeks following the enactment brought forth notifications of intent to operate such journeys from seven operators, offering a total of eight scheduled services. All services would compete with existing National Express services, although this varied in relation to both the extent of route duplication and the level of service provided by the public sector operator. The three routes proposed from east Lincolnshire, the most rural part of the region, at least equalled the National Express (low) service frequency, and also offered timings which facilitated day return journeys. On the other hand, four routes proposed by independents on the Nottingham-Leicester-London corridor each proposed one return journey per day in contrast with at least eight per day by the established operator.

Low fares were offered. Barton Transport, for example, as part of British Coachways, began their Nottingham to London service at £3 single, £6 return. This compared with the existing National Express scale of £5.60 single, £6.20 day return and £10.10 period return. Comparable British Rail 2nd Class fares were £10.70, £11.30 and £19.90 respectively. However, National Express immediately matched the Barton fare and also introduced cheap fares along the rest of the M1 corridor, providing the other major cities of the region (Derby, Leicester and Northampton) with similar offers. Rather more limted fare reductions were introduced on the network of services in Lincolnshire (see Section 3.3.3). Market pricing to combat competition was thus most acute along the motorway axis, linking the region's main centres of population with the capital.

The above response on the M1 corridor by National Express, and the launching of British Coachways in open competition, was sufficient for the other three independents offering a similar service either to not enter the market or else withdraw almost immediately. By contrast, the three Lincolnshire operators, offering cheaper fares than National Express, did commence and have survived to the present day. They have not, at any time, met a major competitive response from National Express. Both Hogg and Elsey (Boston-Spalding-London) have built up their operation to a once daily service, whilst Applebys (Grimsby-London) operate on Fridays, Saturdays and Sundays.

One should again emphasize that Lincolnshire is one of England's most sparsely populated counties. If the apparent success of such operations suggest a market opportunity for small independents elsewhere, comparison with the rest of the country does not substantiate this. Daily services to London from rural hinterlands, such as characterize the Hogg and Elsey operations from Boston (population 26,000), are very hard to find. Given also the virtually identical routes and timings of these two operators, one must wonder whether personal pride more than economic logic dictates this particular situation.

The remaining routes to London were provided by Bartons (British Coachways). The service from Nottingham, via Leicester and Northampton has already been mentioned. A second route originally commenced at Grantham, serving the small towns of Melton Mowbray, Oakham and Stamford, along with the expanding city of Peterborough. In mid 1982 the former, serving three large settlements of collectively just over 1 million persons, but facing the steady expansion of National Express services, was withdrawn due to poor patronage. The latter route struggled on into 1983, with several route revisions, before finally ceasing. The changes concentrated more on serving the three small towns (and other minor locations), where no National Express services were provided, rather than Peterborough and Grantham, where strong competition from National Express and/or British Rail must inevitably have been encountered.

Since the initial flurry of activity on London services, only one other operator has sought to enter the market. This was the introduction by G.K. Kinch of a 24 seat executive coach between Nottingham, Loughborough, Leicester and London. Launched in November 1981 the service ran for approximately six months before withdrawal due to unsatisfactory loads. It represents the only example of 'up market' coaching to have been attempted on regular express services in the region to date. The service offered continental breakfast, drinks, video, toilet, radio telephone and a very high level of overall comfort. Loadings during the rail strikes of early 1982 were extremely promising, but were not retained. Certainly, the 'executive' market was not enticed away from car or train other than during this period.

The operator blamed the inadequate frequency of service (again the typical pattern of one return journey per day) and marketing mistakes (lack of travel agents) for the demise. This failure and the lack of interest by other operators in the region may suggest a further limiting factor on the growth of luxury services in this market (see Section 2.2.2). A common link between those operations which have succeeded is that distances travelled are generally around 200 miles and above. This point applies to independent services *and* the deployment of Rapides by National Express. One ought to add, in the case of Kinch, that the executive coach was an extreme version of upmarket travel. Reducing capacity to just 24 passengers demands consistently high load factors, especially if the fare is pitched close to that of conventional coaches with a carrying capacity of around 49.

Little competition has taken place on year round services to other destinations. Even amongst those operators who have innovated and succeeded, there is no intention of seeking further expansion. The only other significant outbreak of competition was something of a force of circumstance. This relates to the services between Corby and Scotland. Before deregulation, the operation was provided by joint agreement between National Express, the Scottish Bus Group and Barton Transport. Due to Barton's involvement with British Coachways this alliance became untenable and from early 1981 the company decided to operate its own services. The public sector operators decided on a similar course of action, effectively doubling the capacity. The greater market presence of the latter ultimately forced Barton Transport to withdraw its services in 1983.

The outcome of competition on regular year round express in the East Midlands follows the nationwide pattern. A rapid return to stability after initial duplication of routes; very limited success for independent operators; and the revitalisation of National Express are all in evidence. Detailed service analysis of National Express operations is contained in Section 3.3.3. Deregulation of express has not however been a non-event for much of the independent sector. A considerable indication of their activity in the seasonal express market has already been given in Section 3.2. On the following pages, we give further evidence of these changes in the form of an analysis of Traffic Commissioners records.

3.3.2 NOTIFICATION OF NEW SERVICES

This section is based upon an analysis of the records of the East Midlands area Traffic Commissioner. Since it remains a legal requirement to notify this authority of any new express service with an origin in the region, we are able to gain a good appreciation of the nature and level of activity since deregulation. There are, however, several shortcomings. Notification does not necessarily imply that the service ever commenced (as illustrated in the previous section). Where a service has begun, we have no knowledge from the records of its duration. A further problem is the definition of a *new* service. This varies from a genuine innovation - a route never before operated - to a minor modification of, perhaps, pick up points, or even the transference of a route from one operator to another. Nevertheless, we suggest that trends in the level of activity *per se* can reasonably be deduced.

Table 18 shows the number of notifications for the first three years following deregulation. The 1982/83 figure includes some 19 seasonal express routes transferred by National Express to the subsidiary companies in the region as part of internal management restructuring within the National Bus Company. Even so, it is clear that the aim of deregulation as a competitive stimulus has been achieved, although the number of notifications have been falling. The Table also categorises new services by type of operation. The dominance of summer seasonal routes is clear. Most are typified by operation on a limited number of peak summer Saturdays only. Their impact on the travel market as a whole has undoubtedly been slight (hence the conspicuous lack of publicity). However, in terms of sharpening competition between two small private companies, the effects on an individual operator, as reported elsewhere in this report, can be considerable.

Table 18

Notification of New Express Services to the
East Midlands Traffic Commissioners

Type of Operation	Number of Notifications following Deregulation		
	1980/1	1981/2	1982/3
Summer only	43	45	43
Infrequent year round services	11	7	0
Frequent year round services	11	8	7
Total	65	60	50

Table 19 shows the breakdown of new services divided between public and private operators. Here we perceive that the major changes in terms of new notifications were made by the independent sector. They account for 63% of the total throughout the period, which can be increased to 70% if we exclude the transfer of seasonal express within the National Bus Company. This balance does not hold in relation to all types of service. Whilst the independents dominate on seasonal routes, National Express are responsible for 70% of services within the frequent category. This again illustrates a recurring theme of deregulation. Rather than bringing about significant change in the respective roles of the public and private sector companies, the reverse has been the case. Greater focussing of intent has taken place, especially if we also incorporate, as part of this development, the transfer of National Bus Company seasonal services to the *local* operating subsidiaries.

Table 19

East Midlands Notifications: Analysis by Type of Operator

| | **Number of Notifications in:** | | | | | |
| | 1980/1 | | 1981/2 | | 1982/3 | |
	Private Sector	*National Bus Co.*	*Private Sector*	*National Bus Co.*	*Private Sector*	*National Bus Co.*
Summer only	36	7	34	11	21	22
Infrequent year round	6	5	5	2	0	0
Frequent year round	5	6	1	7	2	5
Total: Private Sector	47		40		23	
Total: National Bus Co.		18		20		27

Note to tables 18 and 19:   Infrequent services defined as operating on less than three days per week

Within the private sector, there is further evidence to support the above view. Table 20 shows that, in the context of mainly seasonal express, the market is dominated by a limited number of firms. The five listed account for over 60% of notifications in each of the three years, with the figure for 1982/83 being 82%. The latter may be slightly over inflated. Discussions with officials of the Traffic Commissioners office suggested that a number of smaller firms may have ceased notifying - especially with regard to minor service changes. Even so, the evidence reveals that only 12% of independent operators had made a notification within the first year of deregulation, rising to 16% at the end of the second. The last figure corresponds with the findings of the independent operators postal survey (Section 3.2.1). Moreover, the total number of private operators making notifications has fallen from 18 (1980/81) to 15 (1981/82) and 7 (1982/83).

Table 20

East Midlands Notifications: Analysis by Company

| | Number of Notifications in: | | | |
	1980/81	1981/82	1982/83	Total
Independent Sector				
Bartons	18	10	4	32
Howletts	6	0	3	9
Skills	0	4	0	4
Applebys	5	4	6	15
Viking	0	7	6	13
Others	18	15	4	37
Total	47	40	23	110
National Bus Co				
National Express	15	16	8	39
United Counties	3	3	7	13
East Midland	0	0	3	3
Trent	0	0	7	7
Midland Red(East)	0	0	2	2
Lincolnshire	0	1	0	1
Total	18	20	27	65

Finally, we examine the destinations of the new services. These are shown in Table 21. In view of the high proportion of summer services, it is not surprising that most are to seaside destinations. This also emphasizes that many notifications can be summarised as 'more of the same'. They often represent the duplication of operators serving a destination and/or a change (extension) to the catchment area in the East Midlands area. Services being notified for all year round operation show a different perspective - the focus being very much on the major centres of population. The dominance of the National Bus Company in this market is again confirmed. A detailed analysis of National Express services therefore follows.

Table 21
East Midlands Notifications: Analysis by Destination

		Number of Notifications							
		Summer Services			*Year Round Services*			*National Bus Co.*	*Independent*
	Total	*1980/1*	*81/2*	*82/3*	*1980/1*	*81/2*	*82/3*		
Destination									
London	24	0	0	0	12	7	5	13	11
Lincolnshire Coast	24	10	7	6	1	0	0	9	15
South West	21	2	10	7	0	2	0	3	18
Blackpool and Lancashire	20	6	4	7	2	0	1	7	13
East Anglian Coast	19	5	7	7	0	0	0	5	14
Hants/Dorset Coast	18	5	8	5	0	0	0	3	15
Yorkshire Coast	13	6	3	4	0	0	0	3	10
North Wales	7	3	1	3	0	0	0	6	11
Glasgow/Aberdeen	5	0	0	0	2	3	0	2	3
Birmingham	4	0	0	0	2	2	0	3	1
Others	20	6	4	5	3	1	1	9	11

3.3.3 NATIONAL EXPRESS : DETAILED SERVICE ANALYSIS

The objective here is to describe the performance of National Express in the East Midlands region since deregulation. Obviously, it would be cumbersome to produce a detailed gazetteer on a place by place basis. However, it is important to disaggregate changes down to the level of individual locations and types of route. We therefore present our analysis by reference to a representative sample of locations, including large cities, smaller towns and villages.

i Level of Service

An understanding of the impact of deregulation can be gained from an analysis of the level of advertised departures at different locations. This has been carried out using National Express timetables from summer 1978 to the beginning of 1984. Some results are contained in Table 22.

The first point to note is the large variation in service changes at different locations. The period since the enactment has seen an increased number of departures at Nottingham and Derby (the first and third largest cities in the region respectively). This contrasts with service cutbacks at most others. Of the other five locations listed, only Lincoln shows a modest gain in the number of departures. This is illustrated diagrammatically in Figures 1 and 2 using index numbers, with the period immediately before deregulation being set to 100.

The analysis encapsulates the significant change in the character of National Express services. The focus upon trunk routes, combined with an objective of maximizing operating speeds (vehicle utilisation), make changes of this nature inevitable. A competitive operating environment, without any encouragement to cross subsidy, is clearly the catalyst. Essentially, we have witnessed a redeployment of the resources at the disposal of National Express.

It is true that the trends in National Express operations were moving slowly in this direction before the 1980 Act, and that many of the revisions introduced in the 1980/81 timetable were as a response to the CoachMAP exercise. In this sense, one might suggest that the changes shown reflect an inevitable market readjustment. This seems a little too simplistic. Further reference to Figures 1 and 2 reveals that the changes introduced in 1980/81 were not once and for all revisions. Services since that time have continued to evolve in a manner significantly different from those in preceding years.

Deregulation of express coach services in Britain

Table 22
Total Number of Scheduled Departures per Week by National Express

	Summer 1978	1979	1980	1981	1982	1983
	Winter 78/79	79/80	80/81	81/82	82/83	83/84
from						
Nottingham	274	244	233	277	334	351
	216	177	161	262	282	371
Derby	121	133	113	152	179	189
	105	99	100	196	161	191
Lincoln	118	124	89	94	86	94
	59	43	44	44	54	51
Mansfield	119	130	132	105	118	111
	93	92	71	85	80	65
Mablethorpe	66	60	46	34	33	24
	10	7	7	4	4	4
Quorn	60	56	68	42	42	42
	40	42	42	42	35	14
Loughborough	113	117	131	75	88	59
	98	96	80	84	70	30

Notes: i   * The 1982/83 winter period saw two timetables (19/9/82 - 22/1/83 and 23/1/83 - 22/5/83). The figures shown here represent an unweighted average of the departures in each period. 1983/84 analysis is based on the 18/9/83 - 21/1/84 timetable only.

ii   The analysis does not include services which terminate less than 30 miles from the point of departure; for example, a service from Loughborough to Nottingham.

iii   Each row of the table should be read individually in order to eliminate seasonal variations.

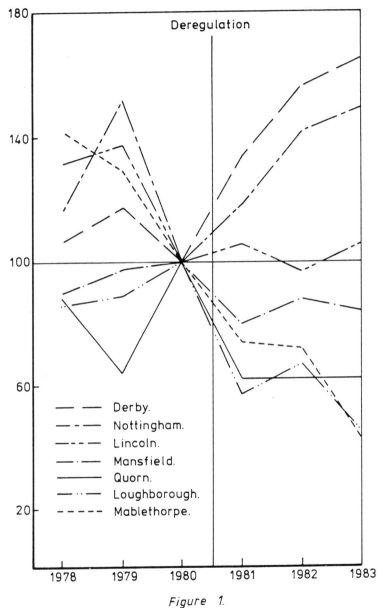

180

Deregulation

140

100

60

20

— — Derby.
—·— Nottingham.
—--— Lincoln.
—·— Mansfield.
———— Quorn.
—··— Loughborough.
----- Mablethorpe.

1978   1979   1980   1981   1982   1983

Figure 1.

National Express Departures - Summer

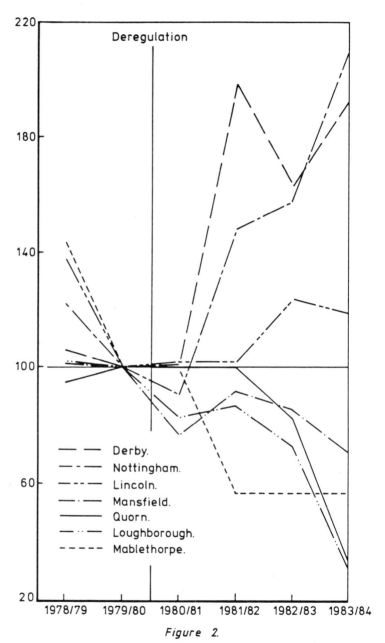

Figure 2.

National Express Departures - Winter

More detailed evidence of these changes is shown in Tables 23 and 24. These should be viewed together, given the obvious contrasts which can be made. Most of the early emphasis at Nottingham is associated with the development of London services. Many other links, even at this location, showed contraction for some time after deregulation. However, having established supremacy on services to the capital, other corridors have subsequently seen expansion. At the end of our period of analysis, seasonal holiday routes and journeys to the Lincolnshire coast were the only services with a lower level of provision than before the legislation. The Loughborough situation provides a stark contrast. By the end of 1983, only one daily cross country link remained (Lincoln-Cheltenham), along with a very severely contracted London service.

To summarise, it can be deduced that the level of coach activity in the region as a whole has increased. If we were to weight the gains and losses to the various settlements by their populations, we should see an overall increase in service provision. However, it does seem crucial to emphasize that we have witnessed a *net* gain. The settlements which are shown as experiencing a decline include not only the village of Quorn and the small Lincolnshire coast settlement of Mablethorpe (6,500 population), but also the towns of Loughborough and Mansfield. Each contain in excess of 50,000 inhabitants. The former possesses a medium sized University, whilst the latter is the largest town in Britain without a local railway station. National Express services have evolved significantly towards the limited stop inter-city trunk service, traditionally associated with British Rail.

ii Fares
The variations in service provision are, to a considerable degree, complemented by a major increase in market pricing. To suggest that low fares were introduced to all routes with the dawn of deregulation is simply erroneous. Equally, subsequent changes in fare levels have not been uniform. To clarify these points, a sample of four types of route have been assembled. These are shown in Table 25 and illustrated diagrammatically as Figure 3.

Although the figures quoted are generally robust, some clarification of the method used to calculate the index should be given to enable accurate interpretation. Difficulties arise, given that various types of fare have been available at different times and on

Table 23
Scheduled Departures per Week from Nottingham
by National Express 1978-84

Destination	1978	78/79	1979	79/80	1980	80/81	1981	81/82	1982	82/83	1983	83/84
London	63	66	70	66	70	61	91	73	91	80	91	59
North East England and Scotland	14	8	14	8	14	8	10	17	19	26	13	46
Yorkshire and Humberside	24	28	37	28	34	21	36	49	43	41	64	80
North West England	42	42	14	14	14	21	42	35	42	35	35	42
Birmingham and South West England	43	27	33	25	34	18	35	50	64	50	57	49
Southern England	25	22	25	22	25	22	31	31	47	43	62	74
East Anglia	24	18	13	11	10	10	7	7	7	7	14	21
East Coast	21	5	21	3	15	0	14	0	8	0	5	0
Seasonal holiday destinations	18	0	17	0	17	0	11	0	13	0	10	0

Totals

Summer	274	244	233	277	334	351
Winter	216	177	161	262	282	371

Notes: 1983/84 reduction in London service is misleading. It arises from the withdrawal of 'stopping' service no.455. Fast motorway services remained unchanged. See also notes i and ii of Table 22.

Table 24

Scheduled Departures per Week from Loughborough
by National Express 1978-84

Destination	1978	78/79	1979	79/80	1980	80/81	1981	81/82	1982	82/83	1983	83/84
London	63	63	63	63	63	23	21	21	21	14	21	16
North East England and Scotland	4	1	5	2	3	0	0	0	0	0	0	0
Yorkshire and Humberside	7	7	7	7	7	14	14	14	21	21	17	14
North West England	0	0	0	0	0	0	0	0	0	0	0	0
Birmingham and South West England	22	9	18	7	16	14	14	14	14	11	7	7
Southern England	14	14	14	14	21	19	14	21	21	21	14	0
East Anglia	1	4	7	3	4	3	0	0	0	0	0	0
Lincoln	0	0	0	0	7	7	7	7	7	7	7	7
Seasonal holiday destinations	2	0	3	0	3	0	5	0	4	0	3	0
Totals												
Summer	113		117		131		75		88		59	
Winter		98		96		80		84		70		30

Note: See notes i and ii of Table 22.

different routes since 1980. For instance, the original Beeper low fares on selected trunk routes offered no concession for children and were based on the simple structure of £x single, £2x return. This replaced a fare structure often based on four ticket types (single; day, economy and period return) with all returns offering some discount on the single fare. Towards the end of our period of analysis, the introduction of the 'Boomerang' economy return offered passengers midweek return travel for the price of the single.

To be strictly accurate, calculation of a fares index should weight all ticket types by the number issued, disaggregated on an origin/destination basis. We trust that the reader will accept our second best solution of giving equal weight to three types of adult fare on each route. These are - single, cheapest return available and period return. An index of single fares was also derived for comparative purposes. There was little difference between the two indices before deregulation, but considerable changes in its aftermath. This reflects developments in the nature of 'bargain' fares, particularly the introduction of Boomerang and reduced Day Return fares at the end of the period.

Three important factors can be observed in Table 25. First, the introduction of market pricing between different types of route. Note particularly the uniformity of price changes on the different routes before deregulation. Secondly, we observe considerable variation on individual routes over time. The greatest reduction in October 1980 occurred on the M1 corridor, contrasting with a more modest cut on the Lincolnshire to London axis and no change on cross country links. Subsequently, the first named services have moved closer together, whereas the last mentioned has remained at a generally constant (and higher) level throughout. Considerable variations also exist within this type of service and were present in the sample used to construct this group. For example, whilst the weighted average in January 1983 was 98, the fare between Nottingham and Norwich was 122 contrasting with Nottingham-Portsmouth which had fallen to 82. Since the Act, cross country services therefore reveal a mixture of fare increases, reductions and stability in real terms.

The final and most important point is that low fares, where introduced, have remained as a feature of the operation, albeit with some modest increases after 1981. Evidence of fare increases in real terms beyond the pre-deregulation level is relatively limited. This contrasts with increases in real terms on *all* types of service in the period 1978-80.

Table 25
Index of Fares: National Express
(Expressed in Real Terms)
21 September 1980 = 100

	3/78	3/79	7/79	3/80	7/80	9/80	10/80	5/81	1/82	1/83	9/83
M1 Corridor											
Weighted	86	85	86	95	99	100	66	65	71	76	73
Single Fare	88	88	89	97	101	100	53	54	69	76	82
Lincolnshire-London											
Weighted	83	85	86	95	99	100	76	70	76	76	76
Single Fare	83	87	87	98	102	100	62	57	76	75	85
Cross Country											
Weighted	89	90	91	98	102	100	100	82	91	98	97
Single Fare	92	92	93	98	102	100	100	78	88	97	109
Summer Seasonal											
Ordinary Return	(85)	(89)		(100)				(72)	(73)	(75)	
	(1978)	(1979)		(1980)				(1981)	(1982)	(1983)	

Composition of route types:

M1 Corridor	**Lincolnshire**
Fares to London from:	Fares to London from:
Chesterfield	Boston
Derby	Grimsby
Leicester	Lincoln
Loughborough	Peterborough
Mansfield	Scunthorpe
Nottingham	Spalding
Cross Country	**Seasonal**
Derby - Leeds	Derby - Cromer
Derby - Newcastle	Derby - Lowestoft
Nottingham - Blackpool	Derby - Scarborough
Nottingham - Hull	Kirk Hallam - Scarborough
Nottingham - Norwich	Mansfield - Blackpool
Nottingham - Portsmouth	Mansfield - Skegness
	Matlock - Skegness
	Nottingham - Blackpool
	Nottingham - Bournemouth
	Nottingham - Portsmouth

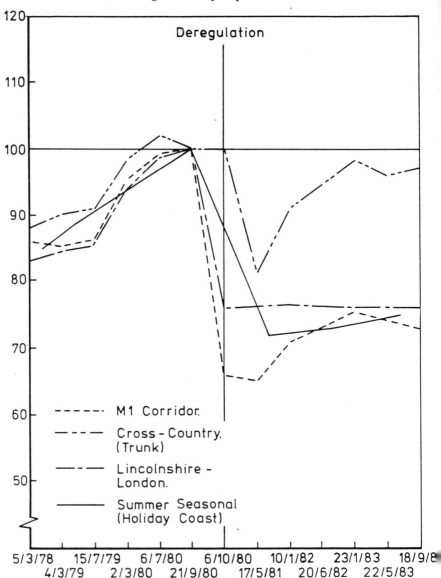

Figure 3.

National Express - Index of Fares by Type of Service.

iii Patronage, Miles Operated and Revenue

Four weekly returns of passenger numbers, mileage run and revenue on several East Midlands services were kindly made available by National Express. From this we have been able to construct a small time series, showing representative changes in each category of service over a five year period. Unfortunately, assembling meaningful comparisons is by no means an easy task. Services operated between 1978 and 1983 have often been subject to changes in routeing and origin/destination. It was necessary to identify groups of services which were sufficiently self-contained to ensure the representation of all National Express coach movements on a corridor, or, at least, where other services (for instance, seasonal express) remained roughly constant. In some cases, such as North East - Yorkshire - East Midlands - South Wales or South West, the continuing evolution of these services throughout the period has made comparison impossible.

Data are presented on seven groups of services in Table 26. Figure 4 enables suitable comparisons to be made. The seven groups include three corridors to London, three of seasonal services and, for reasons outlined above, only one cross-country link. A detailed appreciation of the statistics is left to the interested reader. The major trends can be readily identified. These again reflect the variations in performance discussed in previous sections. Patronage is a picture of all round success. Gains can be seen on all services since deregulation, along with an increase in the load factor (indicated by comparing patronage with mileage operated). Even in the case of the traditional seaside express services, the reawakening of the public's awareness of coaching can be seen (at least that provided by National Express), reinforced by the context of market decline before 1980.

The most spectacular growth is on the trunk routes to London. Given that extra miles run, in the context of fast motorway operations, is unlikely to result in a proportionate increase in operating costs, one can safely deduce that it is on these routes that the financial transformation of National Express has been founded. By contrast, the revenue figures for the three seasonal groups show little or no gain in real revenue terms. It is particularly frustrating to be able to present just one cross country link as a comparator. From the limited evidence presented, this type of service appears to more closely resemble seasonal routes rather than London services.

Table 26 (1)
Performance of National Express Services
(Index Numbers: 1979/80 = 100)

Group 1   **Chesterfield-Mansfield-Nottingham-Leicester-Northampton -London** *Service Numbers: 450/451/458/459*

| | | | Revenue expressed in: | |
	Patronage	Mileage	money	real terms
1978/79	107	101	86	105
1979/80	100	100	100	100
1980/81	197	153	164	146
1981/82	221	190	210	171
1982/83	231	209	241	187

Note: Each period commences with financial period 11 i.e. early October. Hence deregulation falls between 1979/80 and 1980/81.

Table 26 (2)
Performance of National Express Services
(Index Numbers: 1979/80 = 100)

Group 2   **Buxton/Alfreton-Derby-London**
Service Numbers: 454/801/860/460

| | | | Revenue expressed in: | |
	Patronage	Mileage	money	real terms
1978/79	115	106	93	113
1979/80	100	100	100	100
1980/81	171	143	139	124
1981/82	230	214	196	159
1982/83	201	194	185	144

Notes: Prior to deregulation, one of the Derby services commenced at Manchester; another included pick up points to Leicester. As a result, growth from 1980/81 is slightly underestimated.

Table 26 (3)
Performance of National Express Services
(Index Numbers: 1979/80 = 100)

Group 3   **Lincolnshire-Peterborough-London**
                 Service Numbers: 466-474 inclusive

	Patronage	Mileage	Revenue expressed in:	
			money	real terms
1978/79	118	108	90	110
1979/80	100	100	100	100
1980/81	194	124	155	138
1981/82	250	160	213	174
1982/83	301	186	246	192

Note: The spectacular growth on this route appears uneven.
Much is due to the expansion of the Peterborough-London link.

Table 26 (4)
Performance of National Express Services
(Index Numbers: 1979/80 = 100)

Group 4   **Nottingham-Northampton-Portsmouth**
                 Service Numbers: 487 and 488

	Patronage	Mileage	Revenue expressed in:	
			money	real terms
1978/79	118	107	93	113
1979/80	100	100	100	100
1980/81	94	77	91	79
1981/82	126	96	120	98
1982/83	125	101	133	103

Table 26 (5)
Performance of National Express Services
(Index Numbers: 1980 = 100)

Group 5   **Nottingham-Bournemouth/Southsea (Summer Saturdays)**
Service Numbers: 484 and 486

	Patronage	Mileage	Revenue expressed in: money	real terms
1979	76	93	70	85
1980	100	100	100	100
1981	101	102	101	91
1982	134	114	110	91
1983	111	103	121	96

Table 26 (6)
Performance of National Express Services
(Index Numbers: 1980 = 100)

Group 6   **Nottinghamshire/Derbyshire - Skegness (Summer Seasonal)**
Service Numbers: 361, 362, 363 and 434

	Patronage	Mileage	Revenue expressed in: money	real terms
1979	133	98	107	130
1980	100	100	100	100
1981	103	68	94	84
1982	120	79	127	103

Note: This group of services was transferred to the
local operating subsidiaries after 1982.

Table 26 (7)
Performance of National Express Services
(Index Numbers: 1980 = 100)

Group 7   **Nottinghamshire/Derbyshire - Scarborough (Summer Saturdays)**   *Service Numbers: 364, 410 and 412*

	Patronage	Mileage	Revenue expressed in:	
			money	real terms
1979	144	131	109	132
1980	100	100	100	100
1981	120	103	106	96
1982	116	105	114	94

Note: This group of services was transferred to the local operating subsidiaries after 1982.

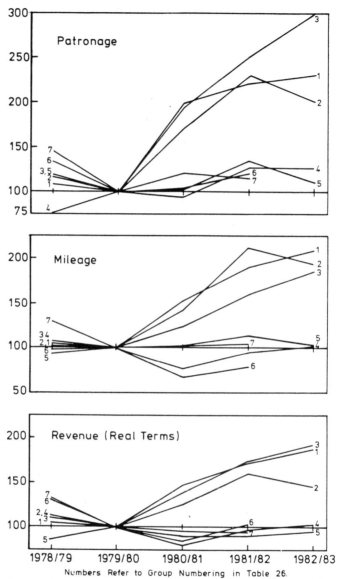

1. Nottingham - London.   5. Nottingham - South Coast (Summer Saturdays)
2. Derby - London.   6. Nottingham / Derby - East Coast (Seasonal)
3. Lincoln - London.   7. Nottingham / Derby - Scarborough (Seasonal)
4. Nottingham - Portsmouth.

Figure 4.

National Express Performance

iv Rail and Coach Market Share

Finally in this section, we attempt to assess the effects of coach deregulation on the inter-city public transport market. We are able to indicate below a guide to the overall trends in market share between British Rail and National Express in relation to the three main cities of the region (Nottingham, Leicester, Derby) and London. Unfortunately, there must be certain reservations about the absolute accuracy of the statistics. Nevertheless, since assumptions were constant throughout the analysis, the degree of market shift should be meaningful. The assumptions were as follows:

Rail: The data collected was of ticket sales at the booking offices in Nottingham, Leicester and Derby. Sales by travel agents were not included, thus underestimating the flow. British Rail's ticket data (NPAAS) suggests this to be of the order of 5-10%. However, the booking office figures were then doubled to also represent journeys commencing at the London end of the line. Since it is known that bookings in the capital are somewhat less than in the provinces, it is hoped that this overestimate cancels out the above.

National Express: Our only data source was on a route basis. Total patronage was therefore factored in proportion to the populations served along the route and the service frequency at each location. In other words, we assume equal trip generation per head of population throughout the locations served, factored by the number of journeys offered.

The results of this analysis are shown in Table 27 and Figure 5. The immediate impact of deregulation can be seen by comparing 1980/81 with the two previous years. Note, in particular, the growth at Derby. Before the Act there was a coach frequency of just two services per day. Journey times were relatively poor at 3 hours 10 minutes and 4 hours respectively. The timetable from October 1980 introduced a twice daily non stop service of 2 hours 30 minutes, which by May 1981 had become five trips each way per day.

Consideration of the last two years' performance should bear in mind two factors. First, the 1981/82 figures for rail are affected by the protracted series of industrial disputes which took place during the latter year. Secondly, during 1982/83, Inter-City 125 high speed

Table 27
British Rail and National Express Market Share between
three East Midlands Cities and London

	Rail	Number of Passengers Coach	Total
1978/79	1,418,432	219,174	1,637,606
1979/80	1,349,832	194,760	1,544,592
1980/81	1,171,896	399,537	1,571,433
1981/82	883,238	479,668	1,362,906
1982/83	1,373,044	476,750	1,849,794

	Derby	% Coach share at Leicester	Nottingham	Total
1978/79	5.9	14.6	14.8	13.4
1979/80	5.5	13.4	14.4	12.6
1980/81	25.8	23.1	28.1	25.4
1981/82	36.1	31.9	39.1	35.2
1982/83	26.9	24.2	27.7	25.8

Note: Each period commences with financial period 11; i.e. early October. Hence, deregulation falls between 1979/80 and 1980/81.

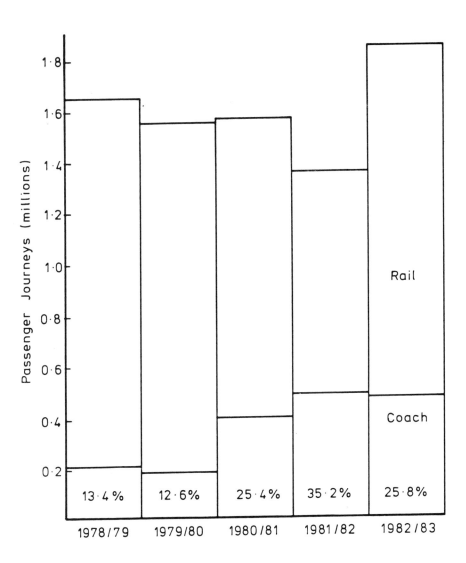

Figure 5.

East Midlands (M1 Corridor) – London
Market Share: Coach and Rail

trains were deployed on the line, with a full service commencing in May 1983. What therefore can we deduce?

It would seem incontrovertible that the gains to National Express in absolute terms have not been transitory. Even the introduction of a radically improved train service does not appear to have eroded coach patronage. On the other hand, there is tentative evidence to suggest that the two operations only have a limited number of passengers willing to switch between modes. During the rail disputes more travellers must either have not made the journey or switched to car or other modes. Similarly, the High Speed Trains appear to have generated new travel rather than abstract passengers from the coach.

We should emphasize that the above findings are highly tentative. One cannot make authoritative judgements without a detailed understanding of factors such as the recession and competition from the private car. The starting point of such an analysis is to ascertain the views and actions of the users of such services, and is the subject of the following section.

3.3.4 *USER SURVEYS: EXPRESS COACHES AND INTER-CITY RAIL*

Having discussed deregulation from the points of view of service provision and the fortunes of different operators, we now turn our attention to the user. Coach travellers were surveyed during their journeys on several operators' services and routes. A small sample of Inter-City rail passengers was also generated. A sample of the various questionnaires used for this research is contained in Appendix D. On the following pages, we summarise the main findings. Readers with a bona fide research interest in further results are welcome to apply to the authors. To begin the process of precis, readers should note that we present the information under three main categories.

i Passenger Profile

This refers to personal characteristics of the respondents and includes factors such as age, sex and occupation. Changes which have occurred since 1980 affect sectors of the market in different ways. The unemployed, for example, might react most positively to fare reductions, whilst other travellers might favour a reduction in journey time. It is essential to appreciate the complexities of the market so that developments can be related to the different groups which they affect.

ii Specific Journey Characteristics

This category relates to information derived about the journey upon which the passenger was interviewed. This serves to widen the study of passenger profile, including such variables as journey purpose and the origin and destination of respondents. This type of data also provides evidence of differences which might exist between routes, operators and modes.

iii General Travel Behaviour

In order to understand the level of change which has occurred, the regular travel patterns of passengers must be obtained. This category of information is concerned with both past and present action, and the reasons underlying this behaviour. Responses to questions relating to general travel can be compared with specific journey characteristics to establish its position within the individual's pattern of modal use.

Such categorisations are not mutually exclusive. Car ownership, for example, may be seen as a part of passenger profile but is also a key determinant of general travel behaviour. It should be stressed that this system of classification provides a convenient method of analysis rather than a definitive set of data.

DESIGN OF THE SURVEYS

The design of the specific passenger surveys was dictated by a number of factors and the relationship between these varied according to the circumstances. First, both time and financial considerations placed restraints upon the number of questionnaires and interviews which could be administered on a given survey. Secondly, the cooperation and assistance offered by operators was an essential pre-requisite to the success of the survey. Some operators were able to provide assistance in distributing questionnaires to the passengers, whilst others found this commitment too great. These differences tended to dictate the precise form of the questionnaires. Thirdly, the services and routes surveyed did not display common characteristics. The survey conducted on the Lincoln to Manchester service, for instance, necessitated a brief questionnaire, since several passengers were making short journeys. Notwithstanding these differences, and the varying constraints, questionnaires and interviews were prepared with comparability in mind. All the surveys were designed for computer analysis with varying degrees of pre and post coding. Post coding was employed where open-ended questions were included, enabling a broader range of responses.

Three aspects of sampling were considered: the choice of operator; the particular service; and the selection of passengers to be approached on the chosen route. Regarding the first two factors, the practical limitations mentioned above demanded a selective approach, within a framework of seeking a representative cross section of services. The final choice was also influenced by the degree of cooperation from various operators. Our view is that an adequate cross section was achieved in relation to all year round services, although regrettably we were unable to carry out studies of seasonal express. Where sampling of passengers was necessary, they were interviewed according to their seating position in the vehicle. The sample was structured by selecting passengers from the rear, middle and front of the coach, and also by taking account of their boarding point.

DESCRIPTION OF THE SURVEYS

A brief summary is given of each survey, including the total number of respondents interviewed, and the nature of the service. In the order in which they were carried out these were:

G K Kinch (Independent) : Nottingham to London.

An express service operating between Nottingham, Loughborough, Leicester and London, offering one return trip daily. A luxury coach with a limited capacity of 24 seats was provided - each of which had an adjacent table. The fare, only marginally above that for conventional services, included continental breakfast and free newspaper on the outward morning journey; and also video films and drinks on the evening return. The coach was equipped with a toilet and radio . telephone. The survey was conducted by self completion questionnaire distributed by the company's courier on the outward journey only, between the 12th and 28th of January 1982. A total of 113 passengers completed the questionnaire, a response rate of about 99%. No sampling employed.

Problems: The survey coincided with a rail strike. Snow, ice and freezing fog caused delay and, in one case, the cancellation of the service.

East Midlands (National Bus Company): Lincoln to Manchester. Service X67.

A limited stop express service operating on a stage carriage licence, providing three return services daily between Lincoln, Newark, Mansfield, Chesterfield and Manchester. A standard coach was used. The survey employed self completion questionnaires, distributed by ourselves and an employee of the National Bus Company, and was carried out in both directions between July 19th and August 4th 1982. A total of 453 respondents completed the questionnaire. No sampling employed.

Problem: The number of very short distance travellers necessitated a brief questionnaire.

A & W Elsey (Independent) : Boston to London.

An express service operating one daily return journey between Boston, Spalding, Peterborough and London. A standard coach was used. The survey was based upon self completion questionnaires distributed by the driver, carried out on the outward journey only during late July 1982. A total of 65 respondents completed the questionnaire. No sampling was employed.

Problem: Coordination of the survey with the operator.

B.W. Hogg (Independent): Boston to London.
An express service operating one daily return journey between Boston, Spalding, Market Deeping, Peterborough and London. A standard coach was used. The survey was identical with Elsey above, and was carried out during August 1982. A total of 61 respondents completed the questionnaire. No sampling was employed.

Problem: Coordination of the survey (as Elsey).

Note: Due to the disappointing response from the above two surveys and the similarity of operation, the statistics have been combined for analytical purposes.

Trent (National Bus Company): Derby to Leicester. Service 207.
This daily service was a short distance non-stop express operation, using a standard coach. The survey was conducted as a pilot for the National Express services described below, using a direct interview approach administered by ourselves. Interviews were carried out in both directions. Sampling was employed when the coach was full. All journey times were surveyed. A total of 62 interviews were obtained on 9th and 11th March 1983.

Problems: A crowded coach and a short journey.

National Express: Nottingham to London. Services 450/459 group.
The service originated at Chesterfield *or* Nottingham, providing 12 return journeys daily. Standard coach. Three of these journeys (service 455) picked up at various points on the A6 via Loughborough, Leicester and Northampton. The survey was restricted to the motorway services serving Chesterfield, Mansfield, Sutton in Ashfield, Nottingham and Leicester only. A sample of journey timings was undertaken, covering the maximum number of services. Interviews were conducted between Leicester and London (both directions), seat sampling being employed when necessary. A total of 362 respondents were interviewed between the 11th April and 6th May 1983.

Problem: Crowded coaches.

National Express: Derby to London. Service 860.
The service commenced at Alfreton *or* Buxton, the latter picking up at Bakewell, Matlock and Belper, before forming a non-stop service between Derby and London. Standard coach. Three return trips

daily were provided, all of which were surveyed. The interviews were conducted between Derby and London (both directions). Sampling was employed where necessary. A total of 352 respondents were interviewed between 11th April and 6th May 1983.

Problem: Crowded coaches.

National Express: Nottingham to Portsmouth. Service 487.

A once daily operation between Nottingham and Portsmouth via Loughborough, Leicester, Northampton, Oxford and Southampton with various intermediate pick up points. The survey was conducted between Loughborough and Oxford, with sampling undertaken according to the boarding point of the passenger. A total of 319 passengers were interviewed between 11th April and 6th May 1983.

Problem: continuing fluctuation of passenger numbers due to frequent intermediate stops.

National Express: Services 450/459 and 487.

We were also able to make use of data collected by the company in a fares survey during mid 1981. Although the design of the survey owed as much to marketing initiative as impartial data collection, useful information was obtained on passenger profile and specific journey characteristics. 1,981 responses.

British Rail

Surveys were conducted on Derby, Leicester, Nottingham and Loughborough stations on the 12th and 18th November 1982. Short interviews were carried out by undergraduate students in transport studies. Passengers were approached on the station platform whilst awaiting specified services. Selection was biassed towards London bound trains but also included other long distance routes, for example, Nottingham-Glasgow and North East-Derby-South West.

PASSENGER PROFILE

Table 28 shows the survey results relating to age and sex characteristics. Considering first the weighted average figure for coach travellers, attention should initially be drawn to the high proportion of 17-25 year olds in the sample. This group represents just 16% of the population aged 11 and over (1981 census). Those age groups under represented are 36-64 years (39% of the population compared with 29% of coach users) and the over 65s (16% of the population compared with 10% of coach users).

Table 28

Express User Surveys: Passenger Profile 1

Age and Sex Characteristics

(figures in percentages)

	Kinch	Hogg/ Elsey	East Midlands	Trent	National Express (1983)			(1981)		All* Coach	Rail
					450	860	487	450	487		
Age group											
11-16	1	10	7	0	1	2	3	4	5	4	1
17-25	10	24	24	59	37	35	31	45	35	38	45
26-35	22	25	18	12	15	20	13	21	19	19	15
36-64	64	36	34	17	30	32	29	25	34	29	24
over 65	3	5	17	12	17	11	24	5	7	10	15
Sex											
Male	73	33	34	45	48	41	32	49	34	44	51
Female	27	67	66	55	52	59	68	51	66	56	49
Sample size											
n =	113	126	453	62	362	352	319	1818	163	3767	555

* weighted average

Such differences are only important in absolute terms. If we are to assess the share of the long distance travel market held in relation to different passenger groups, other data must be called upon. The dearth of good information in this area has already been noted. Comparison with the 1979/80 long distance travel surveys (LDTS) is not totally satisfactory, given that it precedes deregulation and also that the data are biassed by commuter journeys over 25 miles within the Greater London catchment area. Nevertheless, comparison of the age groups of all travellers in LDTS and the coach surveys reveals an almost identical picture. The under 25s and over 65s are only slightly over-represented. Reference should now be made to the British Rail survey findings in Table 28. Note here that the 17-25 year olds share is even greater for rail.

Conclusion 1:

The age of persons travelling by coach is biassed towards the young in absolute terms, but is approximately equal to the distribution of long distance journeys by all modes. Rail has an even greater bias to the young and the over 65s.

Females represent a disproportionate number of travellers by coach. This is fairly predictable given the considerable bias in car ownership and availability towards males. The picture for rail is closer to the national picture (49% male; 51% female), but also far below the long distance travel market in total (69% male; 31% female: LDTS 1978/79).

Conclusion 2:

Women are an important market for coach travel.

Consideration of occupational status (Table 29) reinforces the conclusions reached on age groups. Students represent 20% of coach and 28% of rail users. Whilst this includes 4% and 1% respectively in the 11-16 age group, the remainder are in further or higher education. After allowing for this bias, other categories of occupational status generally conform to the national picture in terms of their representativeness in population terms. By contrast, comparison with LDTS reveals significant differences. The retired (a group which, since 1979/80 has grown rapidly, especially in terms of

Table 29

Express User Surveys: Passenger Profile 2

Occupational Status

(figures in percentages)

Occupation	Kinch	Hogg/ Elsey	Trent		National Express (1983)		National Express (1981)		All Coach	Rail
				450	860	487	450	487		
Full time employment	84	44	27	33	39	30	) 50	51	48	(39
Part time employment	3	9	16	7	6	5	)		8	(4
Unemployed	1	10	5	11	9	4	9	7	8	4
Student	2	15	25	18	18	19	22	18	20	28
Housewife	7	13	13	9	9	12	8	12	9	8
Retired	3	9	14	20	18	28	7	9	12	15
Other	na	na	na	2	1	1	4	3	3	2

persons giving up work before 65) emerge as a group with a high utilisation of public transport, whilst those in employment are heavily under represented.

Conclusion 3:

Analysis by occupation shows coach and rail to be relatively similar, with rail as the market leader amongst the student and, to a lesser extent, retired groups. Such persons are significantly over represented within these modes in the context of the long distance travel market.

The above conclusions all reflect the importance of car ownership and availability. Not surprisingly, those groups over represented on coach and rail had relatively low levels of car ownership. Nevertheless, one should not in any way seek to divide the market simplistically between non car owning coach and rail users and vice versa. Table 30 reveals the percentage of persons travelling on public transport by their car owning characteristics and use of local buses.

The former relates to the question 'do you own a car or is a car often available for your use?' Note that rail users are only marginally below the national average level of *household* car ownership. Car availability for the specific journey surveyed was approximately 10% below these figures. These findings, above all else, demonstrate that whilst the events of deregulation have naturally focussed attention on the relationship between coach and rail, a competitive environment has been present throughout the years between public and private modes. This is confirmed by the information on local bus use amongst coach users, with only 52% using such services once per week or more.

Conclusion 4:

Many passengers (coach and rail) are from car owning households and have a car available for their use when making the journey. Modal competition is very much a three way process - coach, rail and car.

Our conclusions so far have concentrated upon the general comparisons between the modes. Tables 28-30 also allow us to investigate differences between the services. Before doing so, one

Table 30

Express User Surveys: Passenger Profile 3

Car Ownership and Bus Usage Characteristics

(figures in percentages)

	Kinch	Hogg/ Elsey	East Midlands	Trent	National Express (1983)			All Coach	Rail
					450	860	487		
Level of car availability									
Available	95	58	22	44	55	60	41	47	55
Not available	5	42	78	56	45	40	59	53	45
Detailed breakdown:									
Car Owner					33	40	19		
Car Driver					7	6	7		
Passenger A*					15	13	14		
Passenger B*					7	6	12		
No access to car					38	35	48		
Use of Local Bus Services									
Never					16	22	22	20	
Rarely					13	25	18	25	
Once/week					15	11	9	10	
More than twice weekly					56	42	51	42	

* Passenger A = Non driver in household with car available for lift giving.
  Passenger B = Non driver with limited access to a car (household or other) even as passenger.

96

should again emphasize the limitations of the survey base. Individual sample sizes are, in some cases, rather small; data collection varied between self completion questionnaire and interview; and sample structure was not controlled for in all cases. Even after making allowances for likely inconsistencies arising, there are two obvious disimilarities.

The first relates to the Kinch executive service. Clearly, the service was attracting a very different market from conventional coach trips at the time of the survey. Unfortunately, the date of the survey must be borne in mind, given that it coincided with either the threat or realisation of industrial action on British Rail. Further surveys were planned for the summer of 1982, but by then the operator had withdrawn the service.

The second observation relates to the differences between National Express fast motorway services to and from London (450, 860) and the slower cross country service 487. To the latter can also be added the East Midland X67 route from Lincoln to Manchester. The market on cross country is made up of a greater proportion of females, lower levels of car ownership and a higher level of retired persons. This will be partly due to the uniqueness of London (and hence the nature of trip generation). However, although it is the least satisfactory sample, the Hogg/Elsey services to London exhibit further variations in character from both of the above. Other service specific differences are also evident in the next section.

Conclusion 5:
Care should be taken to avoid overgeneralisation of the express coach market. Variations in passenger profile appear to be discernable between different types of service.

SPECIFIC JOURNEY CHARACTERISTICS
Information on ticket type, party structure and journey purpose is shown in Tables 31 and 32. An examination of data on ticket type reveals the importance of return travel. Given that the dominant journey purpose is visiting friends or relatives, this is not surprising. Differences between coach services are again evident, particularly those of the independent operators. The Kinch service is shown to be heavily biassed towards business travel (at least at the time of the survey) emphasizing that a new market for coach travel had been

Table 31

Express User Surveys: Specific Journey Characteristics 1

Ticket Type

(figures in percentages)

	Kinch	Hogg/ Elsey	East Midlands	Trent	National Express (1983)			(1981)		All Coach	Rail
					450	860	487	450	487		
Single	14	39	-	54	19	19	20	37	29	31	29
Day return	71	44	-	(	19	14	10)			(	20
Economy return	-	-	-	46)	6	4	21)	63	71	64)	15
Period return	15	17	-		42	51	30)			)	4
Special offer	-	-	-	-	11	9	13	-	-	4	-
Other	-	-	-	-	3	4	6	-	-	1	13
Rail card	-	-	-	-	-	-	-	-	-	-	20

Notes: Economy return by coach means travel only on Tuesday-Thursday inclusive. Economy return by rail includes saver tickets and weekend return. National Express Special offer at the time of the 1983 surveys was a Boomerang ticket-midweek return for price of single. It is possible that several passengers in the economy return category also possessed this ticket. The majority of rail card users purchased return fares.

generated, whilst Hogg/Elsey show a high figure in the recreation/
leisure category. The emphasis on these two different journey
purposes leads to a common result in terms of ticket type, namely, a
concentration on day return traffic.

This illustrates something of an Achilles heel of independent
operators. The restricted provision of the service (one departure from
the home area early morning and one return in the evening) means
that the clientele are likely to be of a particular composition - day
trippers *or* local businessmen in these examples. The generation of
traffic from the more traditional market segments is hampered by the
lack of both service frequency in general, and market presence at one
end of the journey. Of course, we have argued that specialisation, i.e.
finding *different* markets, is a key to independent success. However,
if narrowly defined market segments do not produce sufficient
revenue generation, there will be severe limitations on the future of
the service in question, and on the potential for other services of
similar character. Certainly, Hogg and Elsey could not conceive of a
viable alternative to London, whilst Kinch did not make sufficient
profit at the fares levied to maintain the executive service.

Important differences between coach and rail are to be seen in
Table 32. Rail performs poorly in attracting party/group travel,
despite relatively recent innovations such as the family rail card.
Business travel on coach services is particularly low. The
composition of journey purpose by coach appears to be changing.
The complete results of the National Express coachMAP exercise of
1979/80 have never been released. However, MacBriar (see reference
at end of Section 2) gave the trip purpose breakdown from the
research as:

70% visiting friends and relatives
9% holidays
8% day trips
13% other

Clearly, there has been a movement towards a structure more akin
to the rail market. The evidence of an *evolving* trend is shown by
comparing the above figures with National Express services 450 and
487 in 1981 and 1983. The divergence from the, admittedly
aggregate, coachMAP statistics is greatest for those services which
most closely duplicate and are provided in a similar manner to
Inter-City rail services (450 and 860).

Table 32

Express User Surveys: Specific Journey Characteristics 2
Party Structure and Journey Purpose
(figures in percentages)

	Kinch	Hogg/ Elsey	East Midlands	Trent	National Express (1983)			National Express (1981)		All Coach	Rail
					450	860	487	450	487		
Party Structure											
Alone	51	37	42	60	54	53	68	65	76	59	77
with relations	19	45	45	27	29	30	23	35)	24	41	23
with friends	30	17	12	13	17	17	9	)	7	7	6
with colleagues	0	1	1	0	0	0	0	)			
Journey Purpose											
Shopping	0	16	19	11	3	3	2	5	7	7	6
Visiting friends/ relations	2	36	51	48	49	58	67	63	74	58	46
To/from work	na	na	6	8	9	5	10	11)	8	14	30
Personal business	79	8	2	8	13	8	5	)			
Recreation/ leisure	12	25	18	8	13	20	8	5	1	9	11
Other (including education)	7	15	4	16	13	6	8	16	10	12	7

100

Conclusion 6:

Journeys by coach are dominated by persons travelling to visit friends and relatives. This is changing slowly as other markets are expanded. The passenger composition on high volume inter-city flows is moving closer to that of rail, whilst independent operators represented are concentrating upon specific market segments. In all cases, public transport is failing to capture substantial numbers of persons travelling in groups.

Information on frequency of travel on the relevant route corridor is given in Table 33. The response to 'previous use of this service in the last twelve months' reveals a degree of uniformity between coach routes. Regular travel by rail passengers was a good deal less. The exceptions are Kinch (the service had only been operating for two months at the time of the survey) and the Trent short distance express, which carried several regular weekly passengers. CoachMAP data (1979/80) concluded that 27% of travellers had not made the same coach journey in the last twelve months. Comparing this with the 1981 figures for services 450/487, we may tentatively suggest evidence of the effects of deregulation, with newly generated passengers experimenting with coach travel. We might also speculate that a position of stability has re-emerged. The 1983 survey results on the same routes are very similar to the coachMAP findings. Such a composition of journey frequencies indicated has major implications for service marketing. It further emphasizes the problem faced by smaller operators to ensure that adequate numbers of the public are aware of their services. Given that 50% of *existing* clientele had only found out about the Kinch and Hogg/Elsey services by word of mouth from a friend/relative, the challenge of breaking into a new market is also self evident.

Turning to the results for 'use of other modes on this route', we find a situation amongst coach passengers which we choose to call modal disloyalty. Only 36% of coach travellers had never used an alternative mode for the same journey in the previous year. The figures for use of train, for example, only drop below 30% of all coach passengers where a substantial number of the individual journeys being made do not have a feasible British Rail alternative. By contrast, the survey of rail passengers showed strong competition with the car, but far lower use of coach as an alternative.

Table 33

Express User Surveys: Specific Journey Characteristics 3

Trip making on survey route corridor in last 12 months

(figure in percentages)

	Kinch	Hogg/Elsey	East Midlands	Trent	National Express (1983)			(1981)		All Coach	All Rail
					450	860	487	450	487		
Previous use of this coach											
None	84	38	34	22	26	24	32	44	39	38	60
1-5 journeys	13	44	30	27	41	40	42	36	36	36	29
6-10	1	6	14	3	14	16	10	9	8	10	6
10+	2	12	22	48	19	18	16	10	16	14	5
Previous use of alternative modes											
None	12	34	42	14	34	30	48	na	na	36	na
Train	77	30	10	44	40	45	18	33	17	31	na
Car	49	36	40	24	35	33	40	32	30	34	59
Other coach	0	2	1	0	1	0	0	na	na	6	16
Other modes	0	2	1	0	1	0	0	na	na	1	na

Note: Multiple answers possible in the case of other modes

There are a multitude of reasons to explain the complexity of this mode choice. They include: vehicle availability; relative costs; the amount of luggage being conveyed; party size and structure; service timings; journey time; specific journey purpose. Certainly, there are major implications here for the modelling of inter-urban mode choice and, at a more basic level, assessing changes in the choice process since deregulation (see later).

To take this argument one stage further, consider Table 34. Based upon the 1983 National Express surveys, we cross tabulate the information from Table 33. Note that the level of coach use does not correlate well with the likelihood of travelling by other modes.

Conclusion 7:

The majority of coach travellers do not use any particular route more than five times during any one year. Considerable modal disloyalty can be observed amongst coach passengers. There is no apparent relationship between the level of coach use and the propensity to travel by other modes on the same route.

Table 34

Express User Surveys: Specific Journey Characteristics 4
Comparison of level of coach usage with travel by other modes
on same route in last 12 months - National Express (1983).
(figures in percentages)

	Previous use of this Coach Service				
	None	**1-5**	**6-10**	**10+ Journeys**	**Row Total**
Use of Alternative Modes					
None	13	13	4	6	36
Train	6	11	4	5	26
Car	5	12	4	5	26
Train and Car	3	5	2	2	12
Column total	27	41	14	18	100

Sample size: $n = 1,033$

Given the above context, it is appropriate to consider the reasons for mode choice. Tables 35-37 compare the results for National Express, independent and British Rail services. With the exception of Kinch, the overwhelming factor is price. Although the figures speak for themselves, we should like to emphasize the positive and immediate way in which the majority of interviewees offered this reason. The importance of a low level of fare is greatest on the motorway services to London rather than on the slower cross-country routes. As explained in Section 3.2.3, market pricing has meant that the lowest fares have been applied to the former.

The strong influence of car availability is also seen as a major factor in the choice of service 487. 'Better connections', in Table 35, relates to a comparison with British Rail. The advantage of rail travel over coach is seen as being significantly reduced where connections are required to complete the journey. Two blackspots in the mind of coach travellers were, crossing London (450/860 services) and Birmingham New Street (487).

Some care should be exercised when comparing Tables 35 and 36, since the survey methods were quite different. The ranking procedure used in the latter asked respondents to rank three reasons for mode choice. Hence, the importance of low cost on Hogg/Elsey may be somewhat understated when compared against the method used on National Express surveys, where the respondent was free to nominate his/her own reasons. Even so, its dominance is obvious. The Kinch findings are predictably perverse, although the emphasis on comfort is hardly surprising.

The results for rail (Table 37) show a considerable contrast, notably the emphasis on speed of journey. Although scoring only 9%, the factor 'no perceived alternative' requires comment. As our phraseology implies, in all cases a viable coach option would have been available. Again, therefore, the complexity of mode choice is revealed, a point which we continue to elaborate below.

Conclusion 8:

Choice of coach is dominated by consideration of its relatively low cost of travel. This may vary in intensity between type of route and quality of service. This contrasts with Inter-City rail services, where journey time considerations are paramount.

Table 35
Express User Surveys: Specific Journey Characteristics 5
Reasons for Choosing Coach - National Express (1983)
(figures in percentages)

	Nottingham and Derby-London (Services 450 & 860)			Nottingham-Portsmouth (Service 487)		
	Passenger category			*Passenger category*		
	A	B	Total	A	B	Total
Coach is cheaper	64	57	59	41	31	36
Car not available	2	15	11	3	44	24
Better connections	11	9	9	12	8	10
No alternative mode	0	0	0	11	1	6
General convenience	2	1	1	9	1	5
Prefer coach travel	4	4	4	8	0	4
Coach is quicker	5	2	3	2	4	3
Good accessibility	5	3	4	0	1	1
Don't need a car	1	4	3	2	2	2
Coach more comfortable	1	2	2	5	1	3
Other reasons	5	3	4	7	7	6
Sample size: n =	236	507	743	163	178	341

Notes: Type A passengers: no journey by another mode in last 12 months
Type B passengers: journey by another mode in last 12 months
25%A and 23%B gave more than one reason for choice

Table 36
Express User Surveys: Specific Journey Characteristics 6
Reasons for Choosing Coach: Independent Operators
(figures in percentages)

	Kinch	**Hogg/Elsey**
Low cost of travel	14	45
Convenient pick up/set down points	17	19
Conveniently timed services	13	13
Good safety record	7	9
Recommendation from friend/relative	9	6
High level of comfort	21	1
Curiosity/to try out service	13	2
Fast journey times	6	6

Note: Respondents were asked to rank up to three factors from the above
list which was given in the questionnaire. Percentages based
upon scoring system. 1st reason = 3pts: 2nd = 2pts: 3rd = 1pt.
Other advantages could be stated. Over 5% of the sample on Kinch
added: no parking problems; rail strike; good personal attention.

Table 37
Express User Surveys: Specific Journey Characteristics 7
Reasons for Choosing Rail: BR Survey
(figure in percentages)

Faster journey time	30
Greater convenience	22
Low cost of travel	10
Greater comfort	9
No perceived alternative*	9
Good accessibility	7
Other (including free/ concessionary travel)	13

Notes: Passengers given free response and could cite several reasons.
* In all cases, a journey by express coach was possible.

9% of rail passengers, as stated above, had an inadequate market knowledge of express coach services (no perceived alternative). Given the unique infrastructure of railways, it is perhaps not surprising that coach passengers did not express a complete lack of awareness of rail alternatives (Table 35). However, levels of awareness can clearly vary between a general appreciation that there *may* be an alternative way of making the journey to a thorough investigation into the timings, fares etc. of each mode. Our interviews with passengers on the National Express services allowed some quantification of this aspect. The results are summarised in Table 38. There is a large element of subjectivity in this analysis. For instance, the true statement 'I didn't check the fares and services, but I know it would have been more expensive' is classified in the low awareness grouping. On this basis, the magnitude of those with little knowledge, and hence, consideration of rail as an alternative must surely be a significant finding, and makes an intriguing comparison with the actual use of alternative modes shown in Table 33.

Conclusion 9:

The decision to travel by coach is made by the majority of users with only limited awareness of the price and level of service of the competing public transport mode.

Table 38
Express User Surveys: Specific Journey Characteristics 8
Knowledge of Rail Alternative (Coach Users)
(figures in percentages)

	National Express (1983)		
	450	**860**	**487**
Knowledge of rail services and fares	4	11	13
Knowledge of fares but partial/no awareness of services	31	27	11
Knowledge of services but partial/no awareness of fares	0	2	8
Partial knowledge of *either* services *or* fares *or* no consideration of rail	65	60	68

Note: For explanation of categories see text.

We end our summary of specific journey characteristics with information on travel to and from the long distance mode. Table 39 shows the mode of travel to and from the coach or train. The results are somewhat mixed, again implying a market which is far from homogeneous. Data were also assembled on the distance travelled to and from the mode and the level of traffic generation at specific locations. The former proved remarkably consistent, with around 70% of boarding and alighting points within the town or city of origin/destination (London was defined as the Greater London Council area). This may be thought to have adverse implications for the National Express policy of reducing the number of intermediate stopping points, especially as avoidance of interchange and good accessibility have already been identified as important factors in determining mode choice. Whilst not contradicting this, it does appear that smaller locations do not necessarily generate volumes of traffic in relation to their population size. On the 860 service, for instance, a comparison of populations would suggest that Derby itself should be responsible for 75-80% of traffic origins or destinations. Given also the greater competition from rail at this location, one might expect the figure to be, if anything, even less. In the event, the figure for Derby is 85%. Equally, whilst there were some 47 stopping points on service 487 at the time of our survey, the seven main settlements accounted for 79% of the point to point flows on the route.

Table 39

Express User Surveys: Specific Journey Characteristics 9
Mode of Travel to/from the Coach or Train
(figures in percentages)

	Kinch	Hogg/ Elsey	Trent	National Express (1983)			All Coach	Rail
				450	860	487		
Local bus	19	2	58	29	28	28	27	24
Car	40	31	7	23	25	34	28	29
Taxi	10	9	1	7	6	9	7	10
Walk	2	18	30	7	9	20	12	24
Underground	21	19	0	16	15	0	12	10
Train	3	10	2	5	7	0	4	1
Other coach	2	3	1	13	10	7	8	1
Other mode	2	8	1	0	0	2	2	2

Conclusion 10:
A wide variety of modes are used to gain access to long distance public transport. Point to point flows of passengers are concentrated upon a small number of major locations.

GENERAL TRAVEL BEHAVIOUR
The emphasis of the user surveys was placed firmly upon establishing passenger profile and specific journey characteristics. It was often difficult to collect further information within the timescale of the interview or format of the questionnaire. Nonetheless, some insight into general travel behaviour was gained, particularly from the National Express interviews. We summarise below data on the use of public transport on other routes, overall perceptions of the modes and, finally, the extent to which modal preference has changed since deregulation.

Table 40 shows the level of usage on other express coach and rail services. The data are also cross tabulated with the frequency of coach use on the route upon which the interview took place. Direct comparison can be made with Table 34, which established no correlation between frequency of coach use and other modes on the same route corridor. Predictably, use of either mode on other routes during the previous twelve months is lower than on the survey route. However, it is rail that is more likely to have been used both in absolute terms and with regard to overall frequency. Significantly, there is no evidence of high levels of coach use on the survey route affecting frequency of travel on others. Indeed, the ratio of journeys made on other routes to the various frequency categories on the survey route appear remarkably similar.

Futher cross tabulations were carried out, for instance between other coach use and other rail, but to little avail in assisting with a useful stratification of the survey sample. Analyses based on age, occupational status and journey purpose produced some clearer, but relatively obvious patterns. For example, students and business travellers tend to be high frequency users; retired persons make relatively few long distance journeys; recreation and leisure trips have the lowest frequency of repetition on an individual route.

Conclusion 11 :

Data were collected on the number of journeys by different public transport modes on other corridors to enable comparison with the overall frequency of coach usage on the survey route. The objective was to segment the market. For example, high frequency rail user, low frequency coach users etc. It must be significant that the statistics defy such categorisation.

Table 40

Express User Surveys: General Travel Behaviour 1

Comparison of level of coach usage with travel on other routes in last 12 months

National Express (1983)

(figures in percentages)

	Previous use of this coach service				
	None	**1-5**	**6-10**	**10 or more**	**Row total**
Use of other coach services					
none	16	27	8	10	61
1-5	9	12	4	6	31
6-10	1	1	1	0	3
10 or more	2	1	1	1	5
Column total	28	41	14	17	100
Use of other rail services					
none	12	22	6	8	48
1-5	10	13	5	6	34
6-10	3	3	1	2	9
10 or more	3	3	1	2	9
Column total	28	41	13	18	100

Towards the end of the National Express interviews, respondents were asked consecutively, 'are there any problems with coach/rail/car travel which either discourage you, or prevent you from using this means of transport (more)?'. The main results are shown in Table 41. Although complaints about rail travel by coach passengers predictably exceed those made regarding coach, it is clear that a trade off exists for a significant number of passengers between price and other features such as comfort and journey time. Not surprisingly, complaints relating to rail and car are something of a mirror image of the reasons stated for using coach. Hence, at the risk of stating the obvious, the nature of complaints (and hence, to a good degree, inverse attributes of the alternative modes) are different. The policy implication arising is that the scope for competition can be further enhanced, if any disadvantage applying to one mode can be significantly reduced. In this context, the expansion of luxury coach services and British Rail's saver fares can both be seen as logical outcomes of deregulation.

Conclusion 12:

Inter-city modes were each seen to possess disadvantages. The factors were different for each mode, suggesting scope for further inter modal competition if any of these factors could be overcome.

Table 41
Express User Surveys: General Travel Behaviour 2
Disadvantages of modes: Principal complaints by coach passengers
National Express (1983)
(figures in percentages)

Complaints relating to Coach	
None	41
Low standard of comfort	20
Slow journey time	8
Poor toilet/refreshment provision	7
Poor quality coach stations	6
Bad timekeeping/traffic delays	6
Complaints relating to Rail	
None	28
Expensive	34
Connections/crossing London	11
Late running/unreliability	7
Often overcrowded/luggage handling	6
Dirty	3
Complaints relating to Car	
None	54
Expensive	14
Unpleasant for long journeys	13
Traffic/driving in London	8

Note: Complaints relating to car exclude persons without household car.

Finally, the most important question. Has modal preference been significantly affected in the period since deregulation? Previous discussion has done much to suggest that, at least, parts of the market are sufficiently volatile for significant shifts to take place. We have also suggested that the analysis of a particular journey on any given route will be a poor proxy for overall travel behaviour and modal loyalty. With the latter point particularly in mind, we present further analysis of the Kinch, and Hogg/Elsey services (Table 42). This *implies* that a major diversion of existing travellers has accrued on those services which have been newly created following deregulation. Note particularly the dearth of former non travellers. Although we should take the finding with certain reservations, there is also an overwhelming view amongst this sample that coach travel is increasing in popularity.

Table 42

Express User Surveys: General Travel Behaviour 3
Views on Travel Choice
(figures in percentages)

	Kinch	Hogg/Elsey
If this coach were not available would you travel...		
just as frequently	86	32
not as often	5	30
very rarely	5	33
not at all?	4	5
If you would travel, would you use...		
rail	50	35
car	21	28
rail and car	25	22
other coach service?	4	14
Do you feel the popularity of coaching is...		
increasing	74	84
decreasing	0	2
unchanged	3	4
don't know?	22	9

A far broader and, we suggest, more reliable view of the impact of deregulation is given in Table 43, from the passenger interviews on National Express. Particular care was taken when asking this question and considerable dialogue often ensued to clarify whether changes were due to 'personal circumstances', for example, change of occupational status, life cycle etc., or genuinely related to changes in transport provision. Certainly, there was an awareness by many travellers of the new environment in which coaching existed. The level of change can be seen to be significant, with a diversion from rail being the largest area from which passengers have been newly attracted to coach. In the great majority of cases, 'more coach only' meant greater frequency of use, rather than attraction to the mode for the first time in recent years. Two points worthy of emphasis are the greater level of change on the fast motorway services, and the fact, that for several passengers, the diversion to coach from rail was done with regret. In such cases, the individual could no longer find a tenable argument for paying the higher fare to travel by rail.

Table 43

Express User Surveys: General Travel Behaviour 4
Change in Modal Preference (Use) between 1980-83
(Figures in percentages)

	National Express (1983)			
	Total	**450**	**860**	**487**
No change	62	57	58	71
Increased coach use	30	33	36	21
of which -				
more coach only	12	12	16	7
more coach, less train *	16	20	19	10
more coach, less car	2	1	1	4
Increased rail use	-	-	1	1
Increased car use	1	1	1	1
Change due to personal circumstances	6	9	4	6
Further breakdown of rail to coach passengers:				
Reduced train use by choice	61	59	64	58
Given up train use by choice	21	17	26	19
Regret need to give up/reduce use	18	23	10	23

Conclusion 13:

Significant changes in modal preference have transpired since deregulation. The major transfer has been from rail to coach. Extra travel by existing coach users has also been an important factor.

3.4 EXCURSIONS AND TOURS

3.4.1 TRAVEL AGENTS SURVEY

In earlier parts of this report, we stressed the difficulties of adequately quantifying the level of change in this area. The lack of any formal procedure for notification, coupled with the fact that the East Midlands area contains over 150 potential suppliers of this type of service, has made it impossible to carry out a level of analysis comparable with parts of Section 3.3. To a great extent an assessment of the overall level of change must rely upon the views of the industry contained in Section 3.2. To help supplement this, a survey of travel agents was undertaken. All agents appearing in the Leicestershire area yellow pages were contacted and asked to complete a short questionnaire. A good response rate of approximately 70% was received, of whom 82% acted as agents for coach companies. Non response may, of course, indicate the lack of a coach agency.

The average number of agencies held was seven, with 18% of respondents holding over ten. Moreover, 70% had increased these numbers over the last 3 years, whilst only 4% had witnessed a decrease. This seems to suggest increased activity in this area of coach operation, subject to the possibility that the result might be suggesting an increased marketing effort, as a response to the growth of competition. It was, in fact, the case that 60% of travel agents claimed an increase in the number of coach firms requesting such an arrangement, whilst only 4% reported a decrease. However, there are two important indicators from the survey which suggest that the above figures also support an increase in the demand for excursions and tours. First, almost half of the travel agents claimed to make their own choice of coach operator, in response to public demand. In addition, 20% approached firms of their own choice. Secondly, the response to the question shown in Table 44.

This response is consistent with the operators' survey described in Section 3.2. Further disaggregation, (Table 45), whilst showing some conflict of views, reinforces the findings. Clearly, the major growth areas are in continental travel (tours *and* excursions) and, to a lesser extent, tours in Britain.

Finally, it was found that exactly 50% of travel agents possessed British Rail ticket agencies. We emphasized in earlier parts of the report that both British Rail and National Express, as established operators, possessed major advantages due to their possession of existing infrastructure, including terminals and ticket agencies. This survey suggests that an entrepreneur fired with enthusiasm and endeavour is unlikely to find agencies refusing his custom, regardless of their existing commitments.

Table 44
Leicestershire Travel Agent Survey
Change in level of sales for excursions and tours 1980-83
(figures in percentages)

	Excursions	Tours
Increased greatly	30	50
Increased moderately	50	35
Remained the same	15	10
Decreased moderately	5	0
Decreased greatly	0	5

Table 45
Leicestershire Travel Agent Survey
Change in popularity of types of excursions and tours 1980-83
(Figures in percentages)

	Increasing	Decreasing	No Change
Half day excursion	12	65	23
U.K. day excursion (seaside)	44	50	6
U.K. day excursion (countryside)	47	53	0
Special event excursion	40	47	13
Continental day trip	72	28	0
U.K. tour	60	35	5
Continental tour	90	5	5

3.4.2 USER SURVEYS

Surveys were undertaken on a variety of excursions and tours, albeit with a bias towards the more traditional part of this market. They range from 'a day at the races', to a nine day tour of the Moselle Valley. Unfortunately, some problems were encountered with the sample. Two private operators, having repeatedly promised to administer the surveys, did not produce returns. Furthermore, one

Table 46

Summary of Excursion User Surveys

Date	Operator	Destination	Number of Questionnaires
4. 8.82	United Counties	The Cotswolds	19
5. 8.82		Brighton	42
8. 8.82		Kew/Hampton Court	39
12. 8.82		Clacton on Sea	21
14. 8.82		Dunkirk	39
15. 8.82		Windsor	13
18. 8.82		Sandringham	35
22. 8.82		Southampton	35
30. 8.82		Snowdonia	40
3. 8.82	Trent	London Airport	19
5. 8.82		Regents Park Zoo	21
5. 8.82		Lake District	40
11. 8.82		Wedgewood Pottery	30
12. 8.82		Bourton on the Water	24
17. 8.82		York Races	8
17. 8.82		Rhyl	36
17. 8.82		Rhyl	24
11. 9.82		Doncaster Races	8
12. 9.82		Kinder Scout	12
24. 5.83	Kinch	Chelsea Flower Show	25
25. 5.83		Chelsea Flower Show	33

Note: Response rate = 71.6%

operator issued excursion questionnaires to tour passengers, thereby invalidating a small number of responses. A full list of services is presented in Tables 46 and 47. All surveys were carried out by means of a self completion questionnaire administered by the driver or courier under the direction of the operator. The questionnaire was designed with this procedure in mind and results are not thought to be substantially biassed. With one or two exceptions, the response rates were very satisfactory, particularly as the high preponderance of family and group travel, in itself, reduces the numbers likely to complete the form. The total sample comprises 825 responses, of whom 70% were travelling on excursions. A copy of the excursions questionnaire is included in Appendix E. To allow comparability with the express users survey (Section 3.3.4), we analyse the results under the same three general categories.

Table 47
Summary of Tours User Surveys

Tours	Operator	Destination	Duration (Days)	Number of Questionnaires
3. 9.82	Jalna	Moselle Valley, Germany	9	44
4. 9.82		Isle of Wight	8	43
18. 9.82	Boydens	Perranporth	8	25
18. 9.82		St. Ives	8	16
25. 9.82		St. Ives	8	20
4.10.82		Sandown (I.of Wight)	5	37
4.10.82		Sandown (I.of Wight)	5	46
29.10.82		Bournemouth	3	27

Note: Response rate = 93.8%

PASSENGER PROFILE

Table 48 reveals a large preponderance of travellers in the middle aged and elderly categories. This was particularly the case with tours services and the Kinch excursions to the Chelsea flower show. One should emphasize that the inclusion of this operator's service was, as in express, due to its considerable contrast with the conventional image of coaching. The price (which was relatively high) included meals and refreshments and conveyance in a luxury vehicle.

Females form an even more dominant part of this market than in express. By contrast, car ownership levels for 'conventional' excursion travellers are very similar to the characteristics of express users. The figure is higher amongst tours passengers, but contrastingly low in answer to the question 'was the car available for this journey?' It is conceivable that some respondents answered negatively on the pretext that they would not use a car for such a trip, rather than in relation to actual availability.

SPECIFIC JOURNEY CHARACTERISTICS

Unlike express operations, which appear to be failing to capture the group travel market, excursions and tours have their strength in this area. Table 49 shows an inverse relationship between the two types of service and party structure. Combining the above with data on passenger profile, there is little doubt that the structure of the market for excursions and tours is quite different from express. The Table also shows that reasons for choosing coach are very much at variance. The low ranking of value for money does not reflect acute cost consciousness, whilst the high figures of 'recommended by a friend' for conventional excursions, suggests a rather stable composition. The most positive aspect of mode choice on the questionnaire, namely, 'a pleasant way to travel' scores badly, although we might also consider 'personal attention/services of a guide' to be a distinctive attribute. Finally, attention should again be drawn to the 'comfort' ranking on the Kinch service. Far more research needs to be carried out to establish the precise impact of high quality vehicles on the market. What appears irrefutable is that the public travelling on this operator's vehicles were aware of and responsive to the improved levels of comfort provided.

A corollary to this is provided in the response to question 17 of the survey where respondents could cite any improvements they would like to see on excursions and tours. With the exceptions of cheap

Table 48

Excursions and Tours User Surveys: Passenger Profile

(figures in percentages)

	Excursions			Tours		Express Coach Users
	United Counties	Trent	Kinch	Boyden	Jalna	
Age group						
11-16	10	12	2	1	0	4
17-25	9	6	2	5	6	38
26-35	9	12	3	5	6	19
36-64	45	47	76	42	53	29
65 and over	26	23	17	47	25	10
Sex						
Male	34	36	29	40	39	44
Female	66	64	71	60	61	56
General car availability						
Available	47	42	83	62	59	47
Not available	53	58	17	28	41	53
Car availability for this journey						
Available	39	37	78	43	43	c.37
Not available	61	63	22	57	57	c.63
Sample size *n =*	287	222	58	171	87	825

119

Table 49

Excursions and Tours User Surveys: Specific Journey Characteristics 1

(figures in percentages)

	Excursions			Tours		Express Coach Users
	United Counties	Trent	Kinch	Boyden	Jalna	
Party Structure						
Unaccompanied	9	7	12	8	11	77
With family/relations	69	77	60	72	67	) 23
With friends	22	16	28	20	22	)
Reasons for Choosing Coach						
Comfort	6	0	31	16	21	
Friend/family recommended	51	64	2	11	12	
Value for money	8	5	23	27	7	
Attractions of destination	24	19	18	7	25	
Personal attention	9	6	16	10	19	
Pleasant way to travel	2	5	10	10	16	
Services of guide courier	na	na	na	11	na*	
Quality of hotels offered	na	na	na	7	na*	

Note: * Incorrect survey form used by operator (see text).

fares for pensioners and better advance information about the nature of the journey and its destination, all other complaints related to 'in vehicle' comforts. Requests were made for the provision of on-coach toilets; improved air conditioning; provision of music; better seating and/or more leg room. However, to return to our impression of a relatively stable market, only 33% of respondents made any response to this question, of whom 15% stated that they were 'completely satisfied' with the service provided.

Table 50 offers information on how the decision to travel is made. A difference occurs between excursions and tours in relation to the method of finding out about the service. The importance of local press advertisements for tours emphasizes the small geographical areas upon which this type of operation is based, and again contrasts with express services. Around two thirds of all passengers joined their vehicle within 5 miles of their home. The latter also reflects the policy pursued by many operators of often having several local pick up points. Those passengers responding to press advertising were most likely to book their journey at the shortest notice.

The response to 'planning the journey', confirms much of the preceding description of the nature of the market. Note the large numbers of persons choosing an operator first. With the exception of Kinch, running to a relatively unique special event, the choice of operator consistently exceeds that of the destination. Questions of mode loyalty and market stability are further discussed below.

GENERAL TRAVEL BEHAVIOUR

Table 51 shows a market with considerable repeat use of services. Note for example that 35% of United Counties passengers had made at least six similar journeys in the past two years, whilst 31% of Boydens tour travellers average one or more trips per year. In addition, we can also perceive very limited operator loyalty, with the exception of Trent excursions. The relatively high figures for 'another operator' in the cases of Kinch and Boydens is understandable, given that these firms were both relatively new and expanding (although both pre date deregulation).

Such findings go a long way towards confirming the trends in excursions and tours reported in the operators' survey. Whilst the market is probably quite bouyant, the expansion of supply may be exceeding demand. It seems irrefutable that the public are being presented with a significant choice of operators and may well be

Table 50
Excursions and Tours User Surveys: Specific Journey Characteristics 2
(figures in percentages)

	Excursions			Tours	
	United Counties	Trent	Kinch	Boyden	Jalna
Method of finding out about Service					
Travel agent/operators Office	68	55	64	13	20
Friend/relative	16	16	31	18	29
Press advertisement	10	27	2	64	43
Radio advertisement	0	0	0	0	0
Other source	6	2	3	5	7
*Decision made to travel**					
Almost immediately	9	13	13	12	7
Short term	23	27	9	31	⎫
Medium term	41	30	9	27	⎬ 93
Long term	27	30	69	30	⎭
Planning the Journey					
Chose Destination first	33	32	75	12	28
Chose operator first	38	38	9	27	34
No preference for either	12	20	9	21	21
Choice made by someone else	14	8	2	27	12

Note: * Categories varied between excursions and tours.

          Excursions: upto 2 days; upto 1 week; 1-2 weeks; more than 2 weeks

          Tours: upto 2 weeks; upto 1 month; upto 3 months; more than 3 months

Table 51

Excursions and Tours User Surveys: General Travel Behaviour 1

(figures in percentages)

	Excursions			Tours	
	United Counties	Trent	Kinch	Boyden	Jalna
Number of Excursions (Tours) in last 2 years:					
None	9	31	31	(39)	na
1-5 (1-2)	56	44	57	(30)	na
6-10 (2-5)	18	14	5	(20)	na
10+ (5+)	17	11	7	(11)	na
If journeys made, were they...					
With the same operator only	27	47	3	8	29
With another operator only	9	18	77	61	26
With both of the above	64	35	20	31	45
Use of other services of this Operator?					
Yes	71	64	17	26	21
No	29	36	83	74	79
If yes, were these...					
Tours (Excursions)	3	14	12	(71)	na
Stage Carriage	81	64	-	3	na
Other	16	22	88	26	na

experimenting accordingly. Further consideration of those passengers stating that they chose the operator first in planning their journey (Table 50) is therefore warranted. These respondents *are* more likely than others to have a loyalty to the same operator, but the difference is not significant.

Use of other services provided by the operator (Table 51) is relatively predictable, given the market presence of the different firms. However, admittedly from a very limited stage carriage base, Boydens do not appear to enjoy any knock-on benefit for their tours. Although only a small number of passengers had used Kinch before, attention is drawn to the 88% in the 'other' category. This could include travel on a private hire, but may also reflect use of the London executive service. Again, one might speculate upon the marketing advantages of luxury vehicles.

Apart from the above, the figures in Table 51 do not give any indication of the use of express services by passengers on excursions and tours. Data on this relationship can, however, be presented from a question put to *express* users during the National Express (1983) surveys. This revealed that only 23% of the sample had used any form of coach excursion or tour in the last year, confirming the separate nature of the two markets. Comparison of this figure with previous use of rail, car, and local bus by express coach users (Section 3.3.4), reveals that the interaction with excursions and tours is lower than in each of these other cases.

A hypothesis is therefore that excursions and tours users make few long distance journeys by other means. Table 52 confirms this for rail travel, although it should be noted that the question relates deliberately to leisure trips by this mode. The Table also shows a level of local bus use somewhat higher than amongst express coach users.

Finally, the question on 'the popularity of coaching'. This produced even higher responses in the 'increasing' category than was found on independent operators express services. Although we can make only the mildest inference, the unanimity of view must suggest a public perception of a buoyant industry.

Summary

We conclude that the excursions and tours market is very different from express. It comprises a relatively stable body of travellers with a distinct passenger profile. This structure is significantly unrepresentative of the population at large and the overall make up of the long distance travel market. Mode loyalty seems high, with limited use of other modes and a somewhat uncritical acceptance of the quality of coach travel. Operator disloyalty is significant.

Table 52

Excursions and Tours User Surveys: General Travel Behaviour 2
(figures in percentages)

	Excursions			Tours	
	United Counties	Trent	Kinch	Boyden	Jalna
Use of rail for leisure travel:					
Never	38	35	57	54	62
Once per year	31	43	22	28	24
2-4 times per year	16	14	14	8	8
More than 4 times per year	15	8	7	10	6
Use of local buses:					
Never	9	3	28	7	22
Rarely	31	26	45	38	31
Once per week	17	18	3	17	20
Twice per week or more	43	53	24	38	27
Views on the popularity of coaching:					
Increasing	72	71	89	79	71
Decreasing	3	5	2	2	1
Unchanged	6	9	-	4	5
Don't know	19	15	9	15	23

SECTION 4. SUMMARY AND CONCLUSIONS

The major groups affected by the legislation provide a framework around which an evaluative system is constructed. Analysis of experience and, in the case of transport operators, their performance contributes to an overall assessment of the Act. We examine the costs and benefits which have arisen, along with their incidence. This in turn indicates the success of the legislation in meeting its objectives. Given our findings that the express and excursion and tour markets are not substantially interrelated we initially retain separate consideration. The former is presented under four agency headings.

EXPRESS

i Independent coach operators

Any assessment of the impacts upon this sector must retain the distinction between regular frequency long distance and other types of operation. The Act appeared to offer the greatest opportunity for expansion in the first named category, where public sector operators had traditionally been dominant and licensing restrictions most severe. The independent sector's performance on regular frequency operation can be divided into three categories. This reflects the actions of the firms in their response to the new operating environment.

The vast majority have taken no action. They have preferred to concentrate upon their existing markets, such as contract and private hire. The legislation has had little impact in this context. Reasons for not seeking expansion have included,

   i a general reluctance to take risk (lack of entrepreneurial drive)

   ii the small size of the firm has restricted innovation, especially into new markets

   iii a pessimism surrounding the effects of the legislation and its likely benefits to the individual firm. In effect, apprehension towards a competitive environment.

It is impossible to identify the precise strength of each of the above factors. They are, in any event, closely linked. It should be emphasized that the last two factors suggest an inability rather than a lack of will to respond by the operator. Removal of licensing restriction cannot be seen as an automatic guarantee of innovation and competition in an imperfect market.

The second group of companies are those who introduced or expanded express services which have subsequently failed. The initiative, in most cases, was on a route from the home area to London. Reasons for failure can be summarised as:

    i intense price competition from other operators, especially National Express.

    ii lack of high service frequency (again vis a vis National Express)

    iii marketing inexperience and inadequacies

    iv difficulties surrounding pick up and set down points

    v the introduction of the service was an experimental method of utilizing spare capacity and a long term commitment was not necessarily evident.

The epitomy of operators who constitute this group are the British Coachways consortium, but many small firms are also included.

The final group of independent operators are those whose new operations have succeeded. Their numbers are very small. In the East Midlands context, they represent only 2% of all firms. It seems a fair generalisation to suggest that they embarked upon a strategy of specialisation and/or consolidation. The former involved the identification of new markets, either by offering greater quality than the competitor, or by operating a new route where sufficient latent demand could be found. Consolidation implies a recognition of the limits to growth. Few operators have extended their services beyond the one or two routes commenced since October 1980. In geographical terms, this means that the great majority of services are to and from London, with negligible activity on all other corridors.

A further aspect of consolidation has been to enter joint agreements with the market leader, National Express. This has enabled problems of marketing to be overcome. Most important, it brings to an end existing competition and unexpected future threats thereto between the operators. It might be noted that such collaboration contradicts free market philosophy.

The impact of deregulation on the independent sector has been far greater in relation to the commuter coaching and seasonal express markets. This has been either in their role as innovator (applying to about one in six of East Midlands firms) or as a recipient of competition. It is difficult to evaluate precisely the impacts on the sector as a whole, for several reasons outlined in the preceding sections. We conclude that there are genuinely mixed feelings (and presumably fortunes) arising from deregulation in this area.

ii National Express

The key words which summarise the actions of this operator are reorientation and responsiveness. In these respects, it was fortunate that the company approached the challenge of deregulation immediately after completion of coachMAP, wherein existing strengths and weaknesses had been identified. Reorientation refers to the commercial approach adopted by National Express, including the reduction of cross-subsidy, whilst responsiveness concerns the positive action taken against outbreaks of competition and the increasing importance attached to developing the motorway trunk routes.

Despite experiments with low fares prior to deregulation, the stimulus to compete on price was greatly influenced by independent operator initiatives. Nonetheless, despite the collapse of major competition, fares on many services have remained at a lower level, in real terms, than before the Act. Other developments have been the adoption of a more aggressive marketing policy, and the expansion into the quality coach market on high volume routes. The transfer of seasonal express to the territorial companies in 1983 also reflects responsiveness in a competitive market, allowing appropriate management expertise to be maximized in all areas of express operation.

Emphasis on the major trunk routes has resulted in changes to both service levels and pricing policy. Frequencies have been increased and new fare structures have been implemented. The result is the company's domination of this portion of the coach market. Although a few independent operators have survived, the steady progression towards the direct inter-city service has resulted in competition becoming most prevalent between National Express and British Rail.

Patronage has shown spectacular growth, although its distribution throughout all the services in the network has been distinctly uneven. Reorientation has not been without its disbenefits. Many lower order settlements (from East Midlands evidence, locations below about 100,000 population) have suffered significant retrenchment of services. This has eroded travel opportunities in those settlements where other means of long distance public transport are in short supply.

National Express, as the established operator, was well placed to compete with incoming firms. Its success has been partly due to the network of services and existing infrastructure, such as coach stations, which existed prior to the Act. The marketing drive; coachMAP; and, the willingness to respond to a changed operating environment, have served to confirm and enhance that position.

iii British Rail

The expansion and reorientation of express coach operations have resulted in an abstraction of passengers from British Rail. This has been most severe on Inter-City routes, often those where the quality of rail services is at its highest. Although this loss of traffic has been largely due to low coach fares, there is evidence that price is not the only determining factor. It was, however, inevitable that British Rail's response should have concentrated upon the prime issue. The expansion of railcards and the introduction of saver fares offered lower priced travel to those groups most likely to be attracted to the coach. The way in which saver fares were implemented - initially on high speed/high quality routes, and *to* rather than *from* London - demonstrates the directness of response to the coach.

The number of passengers transferring from British Rail to coach is around 30 to 50% of newly generated coach demand. The highest figures have been achieved by the deployment of quality coaches. Abstraction does not appear to be related to trip length. London to Glasgow (400 miles, 640 kilometres), London to Plymouth (225 miles, 360 kilometres), and London to Oxford (60 miles, 96 kilometres) are all examples where the coach has been particularly successful. A much greater influence is the presence of good motorways and trunk roads which allow the coach to maintain high average speeds and erode rail's principal user advantage.

The main British Rail response to coach competition has remained its fares policy. A gradual evolution of other responses can also be identified. Notable amongst these has been the impetus towards faster timings on Inter-City services and attempts to offer improved comfort, for example, the redeployment of High Speed Trains, and the all first class London to Scotland nightrider. British Rail's own research, reproduced elsewhere in this report, suggests that several saver schemes cover their long run marginal costs. The generation of additional travel demand has, in some cases, been highly successful.

Despite this, the fact remains that British Rail has suffered a financial loss from deregulation. This has occurred on both the highest quality/high speed Inter-City routes and the high cost London commuter network.

iv The long distance traveller

The general reduction in the price of inter-city travel (coach and rail) has offered enhanced travel opportunities to many travellers. Price sensitive groups such as students and senior citizens have inevitably been best served. Off peak users have been offered the greatest potential benefits, especially on British Rail. Group travel has not been encouraged to the same extent, with the exception of British Rail's family railcard. Hence, user surveys revealed that public transport was failing to attract regular travellers of this kind. The emphasis on price has failed to offer significant benefits to business travellers. The two important determinants in their choice of mode - speed and comfort - have not been sufficiently improved (or appropriately marketed?) by coach operators.

The above mixture of benefits and no change is compounded by geographical variation. Higher coach frequency and operating speeds on the main trunk routes must benefit a large number of users. Alternatively, for many lesser settlements (even some of those close to the trunk routes) the choice and frequency of inter-city public transport has fallen. Modal disloyalty amongst coach and rail passengers, revealed to be high in the user surveys, suggests that choice depends on the circumstances of the trip, arrival time, journey time and connections, as well as price. In this context, the duplication of modes on the trunk routes is a benefit, but the reduction in choice on other routes is a significant loss.

Finally, the road user as a motorist: the user surveys revealed very little permanent transfer from car to public transport. The minor benefit arising from this modal transfer should be set against the equally minor additional cost of traffic congestion arising from increased coaching activity.

The picture is clearly a mixed one. The choice between modes of transport - service frequency, journey time, fare, and comfort - has never been greater for a number of long distance journeys. By contrast, competition has focussed resources onto specific corridors. Duplication on some routes contrasts with reduction and elimination of travel opportunities on others.

EXCURSIONS AND TOURS

The market for excursions and tours has changed significantly in recent years. Such change is not only related to deregulation. For this reason, and in order to emphasize the distinction, the summary is divided into three sections.

Autonomous change

The nature of such operations is characterised by a large number of small firms. It is mainly operated on a local basis. Coach firms serve the local community, and passengers are generally drawn from a particular geographical area.

Locational variations can therefore be important. The effects of unemployment (and the recession), for example, are likely to have had disproportionate effects upon the operators of excursions and tours within any region. Reduced loadings which are partly due to unemployment have stimulated a more aggressive marketing policy by some, and a widening of the necessary catchment area for others.

The nature of the demand for excursions and tours has also changed. Continental tours, providing a cheap alternative to air travel, have become more viable as motorways have facilitated such travel. This growth has stimulated the need for luxury vehicles, with better ventilation, more leg room and other aspects of comfort. The activity orientated excursion, pop concerts, and sporting events, for example, may also have become more popular, although this is subject to geographical variations. By contrast, the half-day sightseeing excursion has suffered a reduction in popularity, and evidence also suggests a declining market for the seaside destination.

Developments due to the legislation

The Act has provided operators with the flexibility to take advantage of the changes (or to offset the costs) reported above. All the evidence suggests an increase in activity amongst operators, varying in extent according to the type of excursion or tour. The excursions sector is more predictable than the tour, although both exhibit inconsistencies in their performance. The stability which now characterises express operations is not evident in excursions and tours, with the level of competition arising immediately after the Act being maintained.

The increase in competition has forced some operators into a marketing campaign to promote their services. The increase in the supply of some services has not been matched by the demand. The level of competition also varies with location. The recession and other autonomous changes have reacted with the competitive environment to produce opposing forces. As examples:

i the recession has reduced demand *but* new opportunities and flexibility has enabled operators to stimulate demand.

ii luxury coaches are required *but* the standard vehicle is still essential to allow deployment on contracts/private hire etc.

iii competition has forced profits down *but* the potential for profits on specific types of services, eg. continental tour, has increased.

These help to explain the instability mentioned above. Their eventual resolution will determine the shape of the market, and the number of operators continuing to provide services.

Two further points should be considered in relation to the legislation. The specialisation which has occurred in the express market is not yet evident in excursions and tours and only a small number of examples of joint collaboration, largely related to marketing strategy, have arisen.

The User

The local nature of excursions and tours is emphasized by the survey of passengers. A large number find out about the service from local newspapers and choose the operator before the destination. This does not imply that loyalty to one operator is high. It is more accurate to conclude that the user is loyal to the mode but not the operator. This suggests that the coach user regards the excursion and tour as a unique service. This finding is supported by the evidence of passenger profile, which indicates an atypical public transport user. In short, excursions and tours are commonly offered to a specific and identifiable sector of the population.

The expansion of supply may slowly be extending the attraction of excursions and tours to other potential users. It should certainly be increasing the choice for the existing clientele. Some sensitivity to price is exhibited by users, and an awareness and responsiveness to the provision of the luxury coach is evident. This suggests that operators are caught between the desire for quality on the one hand, and the need to minimize fares on the other. For this reason, it is possible to postulate a long term outcome of competition as a polarised market, with high cost and quality luxury vehicles contrasting with the standard coach. The speed with which this may evolve is more difficult to predict.

OVERALL CONCLUSIONS

The synthesis of our analysis is shown in Table 53. This contains a balance sheet which seeks to clarify the incidence of gains and losses to the principal agencies involved. One must accept at the outset a degree of subjectivity and generalisation in an attempt to simplify matters to such a degree. The table must not be seen in isolation from the subsequent commentary. This examines each agency in turn.

Given the major expectation by the protagonists of deregulation that it would be a blessing to the private sector, the outcome for the independent operators must be seen as disappointing. Although both of the M symbols against seasonal express and excursions and tours are probably beneficial in net terms, the only outright gain to the group relates to the small number of firms who have successfully developed commuter coach operations. In nationwide terms, this is clearly a modest achievement. Where greatest innovation took place (trunk routes), so followed greatest calamity. Of course, this must not totally ignore the achievements of the small number of independents who have succeeded in this area.

Beyond this, it can be concluded that the sector's activities have been largely inward looking. In other words, competition has been confined *between* the numerous small operators who make up this group. The outcome of all the above is that free competition has actually been reinforcing specialisation in service provision and the existing structure of the industry, especially the division between the large and small operator. This can be taken as a surprising conclusion. Several commentators have blamed the market structure of 1980 as an inevitable (and undesirable) consequence of 50 years of regulation.

The performance of National Express is much more favourable. Its triumph on the major trunk routes is only tempered by the fact that it has clearly invoked competition from British Rail. Although it has been apparently victorious in this conflict, the freedom to adjust service characteristics - especially low fares - may prove a long term hindrance. This cannot, however, deflect our major + + finding. The representation by 0 symbols in relation to secondary and seasonal routes may be more debatable. Our conclusion is based directly on the relationship with the stated sectoral objective. Although the potential for profit may not be great (if at all) on many

Table 53
Evaluation of the impact of deregulation
upon the principal agencies

Sectoral Objective	Maximise Revenue (primary) Maximise Passengers (secondary)			Optimum Quality of Service	
	Independent Coach Operators	*National Bus Co.*	*British Rail*	*Coach Users*	*Rail Users*
Type of Service					
Major trunk express	--	+ +	--	+ +	+
Secondary route express	0	0	0	-	0
Commuter coaches	+	+ +	--	+	+
Seasonal express	MM	0	0	+	0
Excursions and tours	M	0	0	+	0
All coach services (net)	--	+ +	--	+	+
British Rail	-	-	--	+	+

Key to symbols: + Positive benefit to agency
                   0 Little or no effect
                   - Negative benefit to agency
                   M Mixture of cost and benefit
                   Double symbols indicate major effects
                   Single symbols indicate minor effects

such routes, the free market has done little to alter this situation. If anything, it may have hastened decline by dictating the reorientation of scarce resources.

British Rail stands alone in the table as the only agency to enjoy no benefits, even in net terms, from deregulation. This is slightly over simplistic, given the passenger generating effect of initiatives such as the supersave ticket. Nevertheless, it is undeniable that the loss of around 3% of Inter-City turnover at a time when stringent demands are being made to eliminate operating loss, is a signficant disbenefit. So too is a loss of upto 6% of passengers on high cost commuter operations. It is also not an inappropriate observation to point out that the current deficit financing of British Rail means that this loss is passed on as a disbenefit to the taxpayer.

The greatest impacts of deregulation on British Rail may be yet to come. It is a well known amateur criticism of British transport policy that many motorways parallel Inter-City railway lines. The implications for future investment and renewal for either mode, currently assessed on the basis of economic rate of return, may be strongly influenced by the events described herein. As this book goes to press, British Rail have announced their Inter City strategy covering 1985-89. It proposes a cut in train mileage of 7% during this period, with consequent reductions in service frequency.

The impact of deregulation on public transport users is seen, with only one exception, to be favourable. On this basis, it confirms free market philosophy that the consumer will always be the main beneficiary under such a regime. The gains to coach users on the trunk routes require no further elaboration. Other + values reflect the increase in the supply of services available. The corollary is the - value for the decline in secondary routes (this also stands as a proxy for the elimination of many intermediate stopping points). By simple weight of numbers the overall effect must be positive, although we do emphasize that this is a *NET* benefit, which is not without cost to certain travellers.

Competition has also been a benefit to rail users. They have gained through lower fares, without significant reductions in service. Such benefits may only be short term. Future reductions in train service, decline of service quality, deferral or abandonment of investment would radically change the picture.

Finally we return to the aims of the 1980 Act cited in Section 1.1 to reach conclusions on its effectiveness. To recap, these were:

    i the removal of bureaucratic restriction

    ii the need to ensure that almost everyone gains good access to public transport

    iii the provision of maximum choice to the user, by facilitating competition.

The first aim has been achieved by definition. This has been welcomed by almost every transport operator, at least in principle. In net terms, both access to public transport and choice to the user can be seen to have increased. Alternatively, there are some major distributional disbenefits which argue against the success of the Act. Access to express services on a place by place basis has actually been in decline, at a pace faster than in the days before deregulation. The existence of choice of mode is strongly polarised around the major trunk routes. The choice in these cases is generally between two large public sector operators, rather than the independent firm.

The undeniable effect of deregulation is that it has exerted a powerful influence on the long distance travel market which is unlikely to be transitory. There remain uncertainties over the long term outcome of several of the events which have been related. It is nevertheless clear that the first three years of deregulation have brought forth net benefits, although these have not been without some perverse and unexpected consequences and a substantial mixture of gains and losses.

APPENDICES

Appendix A

Independent coach operator survey questionnaire (Section 3.2.1)

LOUGHBOROUGH UNIVERSITY OF TECHNOLOGY

DEPARTMENT OF TRANSPORT TECHNOLOGY

COACH SERVICES AND THE 1980 TRANSPORT ACT

1. How many PSV vehicles have you in your fleet?

    Double deckers

    Single deck buses

    Coaches

    Minibuses

2. Which of the following types of services were you operating during
    the year prior to the Act (i.e. 6 October 1980)?

    Stage   *(Please tick the*
                                                   relevant boxes)
    Express

    Works/School contract

    Private hire

    Excursions/Tours

3. Please rank the above type of operations by their importance, using
    the number 1 to denote the most important, number 2 for the next and
    so on.

    Stage

    Express

    Works/School contract

    Private hire

    Excursions/Tours

4. Which of the following types of service have been operated since the
    Act? Please rank these by importance.

    Stage

    Express

    Works/School contract

    Private hire

    Excursions/Tours

5. How many people are employed in your firm as:

    Drivers ☐

    Conductors ☐

    Maintenance ☐

    Administrative ☐

6a. If you provide Express services, have these changed in the last two years? Please specify how they have changed.

6b. What influence has the 1980 Act had on the services changes mentioned in Question 6a?

7a. If you provide Excurisons and Tours, have these changed in the last two years? Please specify how they have changed.

7b. What influence has the 1980 Act had on the service changes mentioned in Question 7a?

---

8. Are there any other changes in your business which you feel might have occurred as a result of the Act? Please include any future changes which are planned by your firm.

140

9.   What is your general view of the 1980 Act?

Appendix B
List of Independent Operators Interviewed (Section 3.2.2)

Firm	Location	Number of Coaches	Total Fleet
R W Appleby*	Conisholme nr. Louth, Lincs	40	47
Barton Transport*	Beeston, Notts	260	260
W Boyden*	Castle Donington, Leics	11	12
J T Branson and Sons	Chesterfield, Derbys	7	7
G W Bull	Tideswell, Derbys	3	5
Butler Bros	Kirkby-in-Ashfield, Notts	10	10
A and W Elsey*	Gosberton nr. Spalding, Lincs	33	35
B W Hogg*	Benington nr. Boston, Lincs	30	32
Jalna Coaches*	Church Gresley, Derbys	12	15
G K Kinch*	Mountsorrel, Leics	12	13
Redferns Coaches	Mansfield, Notts	15	21
W A Smith	Beeston, Notts	8	8
T and R C Spencer	New Ollerton, Notts	5	5
Tricentrol Coaches*	Loughborough, Leics	19	19

Note:* Firms known to have introduced new express and/or excursions and tours following deregulation.

Appendix C
List of Independent Operators in Telephone Survey (Section 3.2.3)

Firm	Location	Number of Coaches	Total Fleet
R W Appleby	Conisholme nr. Louth, Lincs	40	47
Barton Transport	Beeston, Notts	260	260
W Boyden	Castle Donington, Leics	11	12
J N Cheshire	Ibstock, Leics	6	6
County Travel	Leicester	14	14
J R Dent	North Kelsey, Lincs	7	7
A and W Elsey	Gosberton nr. Spalding, Lincs	33	35
W Gash and Sons	Newark, Notts	12	28
Gem Luxury Coaches	Colsterworth, Lincs	12	12
Gospel and Sons	Hucknall, Notts	4	4
Grayscroft	Mablethorpe, Lincs	10	12
B W Hogg	Benington nr. Boston, Lincs	30	32
N and S Coaches	Market Harborough, Leics	10	10
Rainworth Travel	Rainworth, Notts	13	13
Redferns Coaches	Mansfield, Notts	15	21

Appendix D

Express coach and Inter-City rail user surveys

i Kinch, Hogg and Elsey

LOUGHBOROUGH UNIVERSITY OF TECHNOLOGY

DEPARTMENT OF TRANSPORT TECHNOLOGY

EXPRESS COACH SERVICES

Section 1

The questions in this section are designed to establish the type of journey you are making, where you started your journey, where it will finish and any other transport you may use.

(**Please note:** you may tick more than one box when appropriate).

1.   What type of ticket do you have for this coach service?

           Single
           Day return
           Period return

2a.   Please state the town or village and the county from which your journey started.

           Town or village _____
           County   _____

2b.   In which town or village did you catch this coach? _____

2c.   How did you travel from your starting point to catch this coach?

           A local bus service
           Another coach/express service
           Train
           Underground
           Taxi
           Car
           Walk, over ½ mile
           Other (including short walks)

3a.   Please state the town or village and the county where this journey ends.

           Town or village _____
           County   _____

3b.   In which town or village will you leave this coach? _____

3c. How will you travel when you leave this coach to reach your final destination?

A local bus service

Another coach/express service

Train

Underground

Taxi

Car

Walk, over ½ mile

Other (including short walks)

4.   Is the journey:

To your home

From your home

Neither to nor from your home

5a. What is the main purpose of your journey?

Shopping

Business

Visiting relatives/friends

Recreation/leisure

Other

5b. Are you travelling:

Alone

With members of your family

With friends

With business colleagues

Section 2

These questions relate to your general travel habits, how often you make long journeys, and what type of transport you use.

6a. Have you used this service on other occasions during the last 12 months?

Never

1-5 times

6-10 times

Over 10 times

6b. Have you made the same journey in the last 12 months by any of the following means?

Other coach operator	
Rail	
Car	
any other mode	

7a. If <u>this coach service</u> were not available would you make this type of journey:

Just as frequently	
Not as often	
Very rarely	
Not at all	

7b. If you would travel, what form of transport would you use?

----

8. Have you used <u>any other</u> Express Coach Service on <u>any route</u> during the last year?

Never	
1-5 times	
6-10 times	
Over 10 times	

9. Do you own a car, or is a car often available for your use?

Yes	
No	

10. Was a car available for your use on this journey, if you had wished?

Yes	
No	

11. Do you possess any of the following railcards for use on the train:

Family	
Under 24s	
Student	
Senior citizen	
Grocery voucher	
None	

Section 3

This section is devoted to a few questions about yourself, and will help
us to understand who is using this coach service.

12. Are you:

    Male ☐
    Female ☐

13. In which age group are you:

    11-16 ☐
    17-25 ☐
    26-35 ☐
    36-65 ☐
    Over 65 ☐

14. In which employment group are you:

    Full-time, over 30 hours per week ☐
    Part-time, less than 30 hours per week ☐
    Housewife ☐
    Unemployed ☐
    Student/full-time education ☐
    Retired ☐

15. If you are in full-time or part-time employment, please state your
    occupation:

Section 4

The following questions are designed to give us information on your
attitude to travel.

16. How did you find out about this coach service?

    Press advertisement ☐
    Radio advertisement/special feature ☐
    From the Yellow Pages/a library ☐
    By enquiring at travel agents/operator's office ☐
    From a friend/relative ☐

17a. The following factors are thought to influence the choice of transport. Please state which you think was most important in your
choice of this coach for this journey. You may indicate up to three
factors. Place a 1 in the most important box, 2 in the next, then a
3 for your third choice.

Good safety record	
Low cost of travel	
Convenient picking up/setting down points	
Fast journey times	
Conveniently timed services	
High levels of comfort	
Recommendation from friend/relative	
Curiosity to try out the service	

17b. Are there any other advantages of Express coach travel which are not
listed above which you feel are important?

----

18. Please list below any disadvantages of coach travel which might discourage you from using the service again:

----

19. Do you feel that the popularity of coach travel is:

Increasing	
Decreasing	
Unchanged	
Don't know	

LOUGHBOROUGH UNIVERSITY OF TECHNOLOGY

DEPARTMENT OF TRANPORT TECHNOLOGY

QUESTIONNAIRE

1. Where did you board the coach?

    ----

2. What address have you just come from?

    ----

3. Where will you alight?

    ----

4. What is your final destination?

    ----

5. What is the main purpose of your journey?

    To/from shopping

    To/from work

    Visiting friends or relatives

    Recreation/leisure

    To/from business

    Other

6. Are you travelling:

    Alone

    With members of your family

    With friends

    With business colleague(s)

7. Have you made <u>this</u> journey by any of the following means in the last 12 months?

    Another bus operator

    Rail

    Car

    Any other means

8. How did you find out about this service?

   Press advertisement

   By enquiring at travel agents/operator's office

   From a friend or relative

   By some other means

9. How many times have you used this service in the last 12 months (not including this trip)?

   1-5 times

   6-10 times

   Over 10 times

10. Are you:

   Male

   Female

11. In which age group are you?

   11-16

   17-25

   26-35

   36-65

   Over 65

12. Do you own a car or is a car often available for your use?

   Yes

   No

13. Are there any improvements in coach travel which you would like to see in relation to this service or generally?

   _____

   _____

   _____

   _____

   _____

iii National Express (1983)

EXPRESS COACH - INTERVIEW QUESTIONS

1. Boarding point _____ Alighting point _____

2. What type of ticket do you have for this coach service?

3. Are you travelling alone or with family or friend?

4. What is the main purpose of your journey?
   (If "Home" prompt to establish outward purpose)

5. What address have you just come from today?

6. How did you travel to catch this coach?

7. What is your final destination?

8. How will you travel when you leave this coach to your destination?

9. Are you travelling to or from your home - or neither?

10. How many times have you used <u>this</u> service in the last year?

11. Have you made this journey by any other means in the last year?

    No Why do you always use the coach?

    Yes Why have you made this journey using this variety of transport?

12. Do you own a car or is a car often available for your use?

    No Do you ever have lifts in a car as a passenger?

13. Do you know the rail fare that you would have paid for the journey
    between (Insert 5 and 7)?

14. Do you know the times of the trains between (Insert 5 and 7)?

---

15. How often do you use your local bus service?

16. Have you used Express coaches on any route during the last year?

    Yes Could you please give the origins and destinations of these
         journeys?

17. Have you travelled on any coach Excursions or coach tours in the last year?

18. How many journeys do you make on British Rail in a year?

    Yes Could you please give the origins and destinations of these journeys?

19. Approximately how often do you use the car? (See Q.12) Prompt if necessary.

20. Are there any problems with coach travel which would either discourage you
    or prevent you from using this means of transport?

21. Repeat question 20 for rail.

22. Repeat question 20 for car (see Q.12)

23. Has your choice of transport changed in any way over the last 2 or 3 years,
    and if <u>yes</u> can you give any reason for this change?

24. Male or Female

25. Age Group

26. Occupation.

iv British Rail

LOUGHBOROUGH UNIVERSITY OF TECHNOLOGY

DEPARTMENT OF TRANSPORT TECHNOLOGY

B R INTERVIEW: TO SURVEY PASSENGERS ON THE PLATFORM ONLY

Excuse me, would you mind telling me if you are catching the

(Insert next train stopping at this platform)

I'm from Loughborough University. We're undertaking a study of road and
rail travel in the East Midlands. I wonder if you would mind helping by
answering a few short questions.

1.   At which station did you start your train journey?
----

2.   How did you travel to this/that station?

      Car

      Taxi

      Local bus service

      Short walk (less than ½ mile)

      Walk (more than ½ mile)

      Coach service

      Underground

      Train

      Other

3.   Where was this from? (Town or village)
----

4.   At which station does your train journey end?
----

5.   How will you travel to your final destination from this station?

     (Complete 2 above) _____

6.   Where will this be? (Town or village)
----

7. What type of ticket do you have for the journey?

Ordinary single or return ☐   1st class ☐
Cheap day return ☐   2nd class ☐
Monthly return ☐
Weekend return ☐
OAP ticket ☐
Saver ☐
Student ticket ☐
Other (specify) _____

8. Do you possess a railcard or season ticket?

Yes ☐
No ☐

If YES, please specify:

Student/under 24 ☐
OAP ☐
Family ☐
Season ☐

9. We/I will now show you a card on which there are various categories of journey purpose. Could you please indicate which one best describes your journey.

_____

10. Have you made the journey to *(Insert town in 4)* _____ for *(Insert purpose in 9)* _____ purposes by rail at any other time in the year year? _____
    If YES, could you please give an approximate idea of how many times. *(Probe: weekly, monthly or per year)* _____

11. Have you made the same journey *(Prompt as in 10)* by car in the last year? _____
    If YES, could you please give an approximate idea of how many times. *(Probe: weekly, monthly or per year)* _____

12. Have you made the same journey by bus or coach in the last year? *(Prompt as in 10)* _____
    If YES, could you please give an approximate idea of how many times. *(Probe: weekly, monthly or per year)* _____

153

13. *If respondent has travelled only by rail:* What are your reasons for (always) making the trip by rail?

If respondent has travelled by more than one mode: What are your reasons for using this variety of transport means?

----

14. Approximately how many other journeys do you make in a year by rail?

----

15. Is a car often available for your use?

Yes ☐
No ☐

Was a car available for this journey?

Yes ☐
No ☐

16. You will now be shown two cards. The first will be concerned with your occupation and the second your age group. Please indicate which category you fall into on each card.

Occupation ---

Age -----------

Also note whether respondent is travelling alone or with others:

Alone ☐
Others ☐

and sex

Male ☐
Female ☐

154

Appendix E

Excursion user survey

LOUGHBOROUGH UNIVERSITY OF TECHNOLOGY

DEPARTMENT OF TRANSPORT TECHNOLOGY

1. Please state your home town or village and county.

    Town or village _____

    County   _____

2. In which town or village did you board this coach?

    _____

3. How did you find out about this excursion?

    Press advertisement

    Radio advertisement

    By enquiring at travel agent/operator's office

    From a friend/relative

    From another source (please specify) _____

4. How long ago did you make your plans for this excursion?

    Less than two days

    Less than one week

    Between one week and two weeks

    More than two weeks

5. In planning this excursion did you:

    Deliberately choose a destination first, and then
    find an operator who was going there

    Deliberately choose an operator to travel with,
    and then select from his programme

    Accompany a friend or relative who head already
    made the arrangements or selected the excursion

    Have no particular preference for either the
    destination or the operator

    Make some other decision

6a. How many coach excursions have you made in the last two years?

    None

    1-5 excursions

    6-10 excursions

    More than 10 excursions

6b. If you <u>have</u> travelled on any excursion in the last two years:

    (i) Have you ever travelled with this operator?

        Yes ☐
        No ☐

    (ii) Have you ever travelled with another operator?

        Yes ☐
        No ☐

7a. Have you travelled on any other bus/coach services provided by this operator?

        Yes ☐
        No ☐

7b. If YES, were these:

    Tours (staying overnight) ☐
    Local stage bus services ☐   *(You may tick more than one box)*
    Any other journey ☐

8. Are you travelling:

    Alone ☐
    With members of your family or relatives ☐
    With friends ☐

9. Do you own a car or is a car often available for your use?

        Yes ☐
        No ☐

10. Was a car available to you for this trip?

        Yes ☐
        No ☐

11. Are you:

    Male ☐
    Female ☐

12. In which age group are you?

    11-16 ☐
    17-25 ☐
    26-35 ☐
    36-65 ☐
    Over 65 ☐

13. How often do you use your local bus service?

Never
Very rarely
About once a week
About twice a week or more

14. How often do you travel by train on leisure trips?

Never
About once a year
2-4 times a year
More than 4 times a year

15. Do you feel the popularity of coach travel is:

Increasing
Decreasing
Unchanged
Don't know

16. The list below includes factors which are thought to influence people's choice of excursion. Please tick those you think are most important. You may tick up to three.

Comforts of the coach
Recommendation of a friend/relative
Value for money
Attractions of the destination
Personal attention
Pleasant way to travel

17. Are there any improvements you would like to see in relation to coach excursions?
